UFO PHOTOGRAPHS
Around The World
Vol. 2

by

Wendelle C. Stevens — August C. Roberts

Research Consultamt — Ron Spanbauer

Story Consultant — Joice Leeds

COPYRIGHTS

Originally Printed in the United States of America

ISBN 0-934269-01-7

Privately published by UFO PHOTO ARCHIVES, P.O.Box 17206
Tucson, Arizona 85710

SPECIAL EXCEPTION AUTHORIZATION

Authorization is hereby granted for reproduction from this book, of selected excerpts not to exceed 200 words and 2 pictures at no charge, and without prior notification, the only requirement being to credit this volume as the source. Longer excerpts will require prior approval, normally given promptly.

Distributed by

AMERICA WEST DISTRIBUTORS
P.O. Box K
Boulder, CO 80306

DEDICATION

We wish to humbly dedicate this volume to a young man
whom you probably have never heard of, but with whom literally thousands of you can empathize. All of you who
have had a real UFO experience and have encountered the
acute frustration of trying to make someone else understand the truth that you know with the certainty of first
hand experience, will understand what this man was going
through.

Doug Hancock, a soldier in the Army Band, had reasons of
his own for his positive belief in the real existence of
UFOs. He repeated accounts of UFO cases that he believed
to his friends and aquaintences while he was there in the
service. His sergeant overheard him one day and sent him
to the Captain, who not only did not believe his story,
but sent him to the mental hospital, a Naval facility,
because that was the only one available there that treat-
ed people with mental disorders.

Hancock was known to August Roberts, who went to see
him in the mental facility. Roberts had smuggled a small
camera in with him, an Aries V, with an f1.5 lens,
which he had under his "pea coat". When he had an opportunity, Roberts pulled back the coat and shot a picture
"from the hip", getting one photo of Doug in The facility
there.

While in the hospital, Hancock had persuaded a number
of other people there to believe him, but not the authorities who mattered. However he was sent home, discharged
dismissed from the Army as "unfit" because he believed
in the validity of UFOs. He was so disenchanted by all
this falseness, and the early destruction of his planned
career in the Army, and his music in the band, and his
concept of his future prospects, that he shot and killed
himself. I suppose those doctors nodded their heads and
said, "Uh huh, we were right".

August Roberts was taken to the hospital that day by
Bill and Ann Woods, who were also Doug's friends. They
insisted that Doug was not crazy, that his crime was that
he believed the things he knew about UFOs. "But so did I,
and so did Bill and Ann Woods," added Roberta.

Bill Woods was not guessing, any more than Roberts or

Hancock. They were among the few who knew. Woods was also in the Army, now discharged, but while in active service, his job was in the "Special Service" section handling UFO reports, and in that capacity went around with a team of Army men whose job at that time was to convince anyone who claimed to have seen a UFO, that what they saw was some other normal or mundane thing misperceived in some way, like planes, fireballs, etc. But Bill Woods also believed in UFOs personally, having heard many convincing stories and seen the evidence; and he did have access to the Army UFO files in Washington, D.C., at that time because that was the office he worked out of.

We have all gone through some very frustrating times over our beliefs, but his was more than Doug could bear. There are many others going through acute frustration and severe trauma over these things now. Our prayers go with them.

PREFACE

In preparing these selections from out files of UFO
photographs, we have already removed all those photos
that we have reason to suspect as well as all that we
have confirmed as fakes. We have also removed what we
believe are misperceived natural phenomena, and are
therefore left with what we consider real Unidentified
Flying Objects.

These are the cases that still mystify us. In some of
these cases we seem to have enough data on the craft and
its occupants, if any, to indicate a place of origin and
what the object is, so that it does not truely remain
unknown, but we are unable to verify that data and so in
a sense it can not really be known either. Therefore we
shall, in this volume, continue to refer to these unusual objects as UFOs.

Having frequently had the frustrating experience of
miscaptioned and incorrectly identified UFO photographs
in the long collection effort we have undertaken, we
have agreed to pay special attention, and to go to what-
ever effort necessary, to assure ourselves of properly
labeled pictures in our presentation here.

We have selected the best images we have in our pos-
ession of the several available copies to choose from
in each case and will present them just as they are in
the files, unenhanced and unretouched. We shall also
provide the full, or nearest full-frame, format for each
picture first, and then if the object image is sharp
enough to enlarge, we will blow-up and crop from the
best picture we have for this.

While we cannot prove the validity of all that we may
present, we will describe our methods of analysis in
sufficient detail for all to evaluate for themselves,
and to consider our methods and our judgement in making
these selections.

We do not necessarily accept the pronouncements of
another on validity or nonvalidity of a UFO photograph,
or series, without first knowing exactly how that individual arrived at his conclusion. We have encountered
entirely too many subjective conclusions that simply do
not stand up under testing. We would apply our own measures of analysis and criteria before agreeing or dis-

agreeing with anyone.

We invite all those who choose to challenge our evaluation of any of the photographs we present, but only after he has performed enough analysis on the photo in question to know what he is talking about, and is prepared to enter into sensible discussion of the steps and procedures we may take to resolve the dispute for the better understanding of all.

Here then is our selection for this volume.

Wendelle C. Stevens

UFO PHOTOGRAPHS

Around The World
Vol. 2

CONTENTS

UFO PHOTOGRAPHS

Photographs of UFOs have always been the least reliable of potential evidence for the existence of this exciting phenomenon. A piece of metal, a scrap of fabric material, plastic, bone, button or cord would tell us a whole lot more from the point of view of scientific analysis. Even a mark on the ground or surroundings from wind, burning, microwaves or radiation can tell us more in terms of real scientific data that can give us quantum measurements. But photographs are a desirable adjunct to other observable data.

UFO photos can be misperceptions of something mundane --seen in a different light or a different perspective from normal. These can usually be detected by experiment and then proved. Hoaxing is possible but not as easy as our armchair strategists would have us believe. There are hoaxes that are opportunistic misperceptions that can be "bugged-out" by sophisticated technical methods when applied. An example of this kind is the plate that was tossed into the air beyond a roofline from behind a house and then photographed by a west coast youth. Those cost a lot more money to dispute than to create.

Then there can be elaborately staged hoaxes using models, paraphernalia, and special equipment and lighting. These are the ones you usually see in movies and TV and on magazine covers. They are in fact quite difficult to stage and relatively easy to dispute. These can probably be detected more economically than the cost of staging them.

Those who make a career of trick photography say that a successful effort takes planning, time and timeing, a great deal of patience, and many repeated efforts to achieve any kind of acceptable result. It requires materials and assistant labor, more hands to hold and manipulate, and leaves evidence in the form of bad "takes" to be disposed of, purchases to be disguised, witnesses to be silenced, and collaborators who never tell.

If his photos get by all this, his troubles have only begun. He will be hounded and pursued by reporters, investigators, sensation-seekers and government agents alike. They will not stop until they have exposed him, damaged his reputation, and injured him in one way and another until he gets enough and cries uncle in the form of a denial of some kind. Some very legitimate UFO photographs have been finally denied because of this. Then he faces the gauntlet of the UFO clubs. If he is allied with one he can be sure all the rest will attack him. If he is allied with none the attacks will be unanimous. He will also be besmirched and ridiculed by the so essential "agencies of disinformation" -- an auxiliary branch of intelligence -- who also will spare nothing in obtaining his original negatives or prints (as we will demonstrate in these reports).

He will never come out of this the same. We do not say this in idle presumption. We speak for almost all of the photographers represented in this work.

Why anybody would willingly subject himself to this attention for a little publicity or to fool somebody (as there certainly is no money in it) is difficult to understand, and when this becomes apparent they soon cave-in.

The real percipient who has obtained photographs, however, has a quite different motivation. He has a truth that he knows is true, which nobody wants to believe. He feels that he must communicate his truth to somebody, anybody. The tougher the going gets, the more he feels impelled to let somebody know, and he persists until he cracks and gives up--or goes down in defeat.

That is what this collection is all about. There are no winners here, but we feel that we have weeded out most of the losers. This represents a considerable fund of UFO data.

COLLAGE OF UFO PHOTOGRAPHS

The two sets of UFO photographs above are here displayed by their re-
spective photographers. Top- Young boys Robert Krone and Gary Schwend
said they snapped these photos in Bloomfield, New Jersey, on November
11, 1966. They notified authorities and their local newspaper upon
seeing the prints. Bottom- Ralph Nicholson said he snapped these two
pictures of a disc-shaped flying object on a night in December, 1957.
Both sets of photos are from the files of August C. Roberts. We know
of no extensive investigation of either set to test for real validity.

IDENTICAL UFOs

Just as we have a case of 3 very similar, or possibly the same, UFOs being photographed in 3 different parts of the world, by 3 different photographers, at different times, all unknown to each other, we also have the situation where the very same UFO is photographed at the same time and same place by 2 different photographers completely unknown to each other, and each unaware that anybody else had taken pictures of the object he had photographed

One of these events occurred during the Solar eclipse of 30 June 1954 when Dr. Hallur Hallsson, a Keflavik dentist, shot 5 black and white pictures of the Sun near total eclipse, and captured a UFO below the thin "night effect" clouds in all 5 of the pictures.

Unknown to Dr. Hallsson, a West German tourist, Herr. K. Jensen, stood on the same beach near Keflavik at near the same time, and shot a color photo of the Sun in the same stage of eclipse, and photographed exactly the same flying object in color below the "night effect" clouds that rolled in from the sea as the sky darkened. Neither was aware of the other, and neither ever heard of the other's photographs.

A similar case occurred at San José de Valderas, at Santa Monica, near Aluche, Spain, when an anonymous photographer (name protected) and Sr. Antonio Pardo, unknown to each other, shot similar black and white photos of obviously the same flying object at the same time, on the same date, using different cameras. Different labs processed the different rolls of film. There were more than a score of additional witnesses to this UFO Photo event, a number of whom gave statements to investigators examining this case.

Here is another example of the incomplete and inconclusive "tests" made by a UFO photo analysis agency to "show" that the object photographed was a small plastic model suspended by a thread, despite the fact that two separate sets of pictures were made, and both in front of different witnesses. We are informed that that analysis could not have been made from original negatives because they have never been released outside the small control group in Spain, nor have first generation prints been released.

12

IDENTICAL UFOs

30 Jun 1954, 12:20, Keflavik, Iceland, Hallur Hallsson

30 Jun 1954, 12:25, Keflavik, Iceland, K.G. Jensen

 1 Jun 1967, 20:00, San José de Valderas, Antonio Pardo

 1 Jun 1967, 20:00, San José de Valderas, A. San Antonio

At noon on 30 June 1954, Dr. Hallur Hallsson, Jr., a Dentist in Keflavik, had prepared his camera and loaded it with a fresh roll of film to photograph the near to- tal eclipse of the sun that was scheduled for that mid- day. He was standing on the beach with a friend, camera mounted on a tripod and pointed toward the sun, waiting for the eclipse to begin as they talked. When the sun began to darken, Hallsson started snapping his pictures with a spaced time between each one. As the sun went into obscurity and began to emerge again he took six black and white photographs a short time apart. At the darker stage of the eclipse the clouds began to roll in from the sea as in what they call "night effect" at the end of the day. When the sun brightened enough for heating again the clouds returned seaward. The two men continued talking as they watched the eclipse and made the pictures. They did not notice anything unusual vis- ually to the naked eye. The show over, Hallsson picked up his camera and returned to Keflavik, where he turned in his roll of film for normal developing.

When the dentist got his photographic prints back from the developer a few days later, he was surprised to see another object in the sky with the sun, which he did not recall seeing as he was snapping the pictures. This new object appears to move independently with relationship to the sun and clouds. The object is quite bright in the darker sky and is clearly disc shaped, with some kind of dome-like structure or cupola on what appears to be the top of the object. The shape, position and light inten- sity are not characteristic of a lens flare. The image is not an internal reflection in the camera as there is no lighter or brighter screw heads, rivets or hardware anything like this in the camera or lens.

The object photographed was quite bright and had very definite structure and form. It remained a mystery with no satisfactory explanation.

It so happens that these photographs are often con- fused with another set of ten black and white pictures made the same day, at the same time, in another part of Keflavik by Carl Mangussen, which are very definitely lens flares, and are quite different in nature.

14

The Magnussen pictures clearly show the axis if the flare oriented to the brightest point in the picture, the eclipsing sun, and in some frames show the multiple images from the multi-element lens system used. These are easily verified for what they are in contrast with the Hallson photographs.

Strangely the Magnussen pictures were the ones that got press attention and were printed on the front pages of local newspapers. They were even reported in the much acclaimed English Flying Saucer Review, with samples of the photographs. No mention of the Hallsson photographs was made.

A color movie was filmed on that same day, at nearly the same time, over Lifjeld, Norway, from an airliner flying at 13,000 feet altitude to observe the same solar eclipse. The movie film, exposed by Johnny Bjornulf, a newspaperman and two others, shows two large disc-shaped darker UFOs in the sky to the right of the airliner in flight.

Still another black and white picture was made during the same solar eclipse, over Chicago, Illinois, by Miss Mildred Maier, which came to attention some time later.

But even years after that, miraculously, another photograph of what seems to be the identical object filmed by Dr. Hallsson over Keflavik Beach turned up in West Germany in the hands of Herr. K.G. Jensen, a West German tourist standing on the same beach as Hallsson on the same time and date. Neither man knew anything of each other and neither had ever heard of the other pictures.

Hallsson information and photos personally from Hallsson

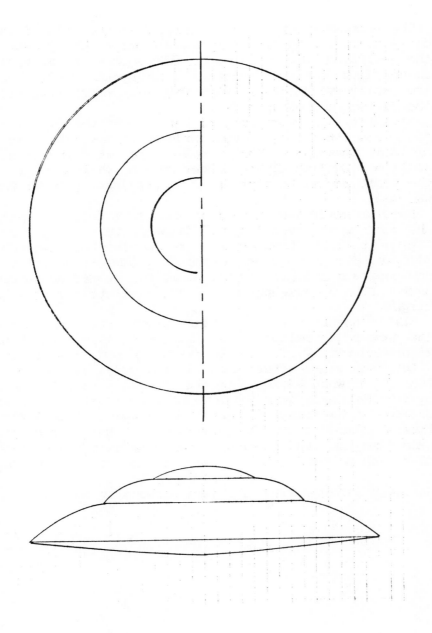

30 June 1954, 12:20, Keflavik, Iceland. Line drawing of the luminous
flying object photographed by Dr. Hallur Hallsson during the solar
eclipse viewed from Keflavik Beach.

30 June 1954, 12:20, Keflavik, Iceland. Photos number 1 and 2 of the luminous UFO as it approaches the line of sight to the sun from the right. Not that it also seems to get slightly larger as it comes in.

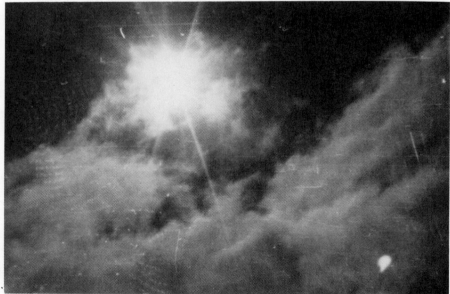

30 June 1954, 12:20, Keflavik, Iceland. Photos number 3 and 4 of the
radiant disc-shaped object, almost in the line-of-sight to the dimmed
sun. Note that the object is illuminated in the near side. If lighted
by the sun this side should be seen in shadow.

18

30 June 1954, 12:20, Keflavik, Iceland. This 2nd photo shows the near UFO to the right of a distant Sun.

KEFLAVIK, ICELAND
30 June 1954, 12:25

Twenty years after the actual event, it was learned that Herr K.G. Jensen of West Germany, then on vacation in Iceland, was in a crowd of people on the beach near Keflavik, waiting to observe the total eclipse scheduled for mid-day. He had his camera in hand and was snapping pictures of the event.

As it got darker and the night-effect clouds began to form, he noticed an unusual aircraft flying at about the level of the clouds there over the beach. He raised his camera loaded with color film and snapped one picture of the object before it flew away, and then resumed shooting pictures of the eclipse.

When we finally got to see the photograph we were amazed to discover that the size, proportions, and the shape of the object in Jensen's picture exactly match the unseen object photographed by Dr. Hallur Hallsson from the same beach at about 12:30 and on for a few minutes. Allowing for slight differences in watch time, the two photographs could have been simultaneous.

As in the case with the Hallsson photos, lens flares, internal reflections inside the camera, and film and developing defects are clearly ruled out in this case because of the structure of the camera and lens as well as their interior finish.

Substantial corroboration comes from the fact that two different cameras, with two different lens systems, and two different photographers unknown to each other were involved. They used two different films (one color and the other black and white), processed in two different locations, even in different countries, at different times. Still exactly the same image was captured in both sets of photographs.

This picture should not be confused with those lens flares registered by Carl Magnussen photographing the same eclipsing sun on the same date, but from a different place in Keflavik. Unfortunately the lens flares got the publicity and few ever heard of the other two sets of pictures of a real UFO snapped that day.

Photo and report from Wolfgang Gunther.

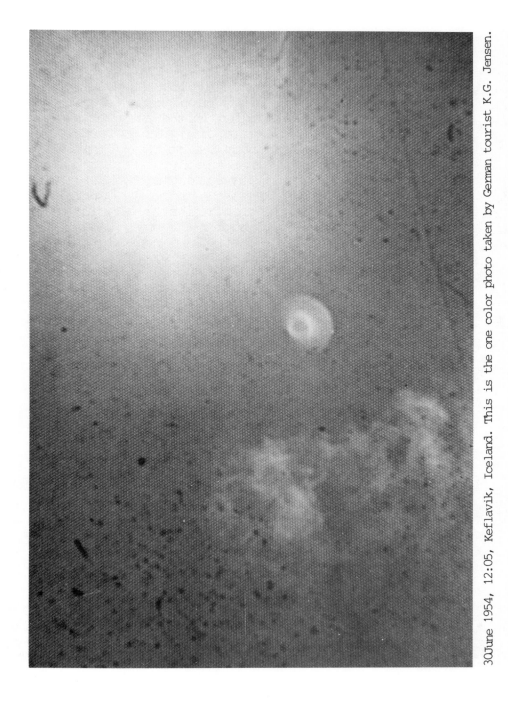

30June 1954, 12:05, Keflavik, Iceland. This is the one color photo taken by German tourist K.G. Jensen.

SAN JOSE DE VALDERAS, SPAIN
1 June 1967, 20:00

Just before dusk, at about 20:00 on the evening of 1 June 1967, a group of summer picnickers escaping the heat in the city were lounging in the shade in a small park along the southwest side of Camino a la Colonia. They were across the road from the castle and grounds of San José de Valderas, where the Santa Monica convent stood. Families and friends had brought snacks, lunches.

At just before dusk they were suddenly surprised to see an unusual aircraft approaching at a very low altitude from over the castyle beyond the power towers. The towers were of the main east-west power transmission line running through the area. There was also a secondary power line running northwest-southeast and parallel to the road. The object approached from the east toward the power tower, where it made a 300 degree curve to its left and passed horizontally from left to right beyond the road but paralleling it, and at about the distance away as the secondary power line also paralleling its line of flight.

After passing the park, it made another curve to the left, back toward the east, where it briefly settled to the ground in the scrub area on the castle grounds a couple of kilometers away, remained a short time, and then rose into the air and flew away.

Two of the picnickers recovered from their surprise in time to grab their cameras and begin taking pictures of the craft. Others were also seen to be getting their cameras out but the sighting was so brief they may not have succeeded in getting pictures. The cameramen who succeeded were at that time standing in positions A and B on the attached diagram drawn by architect Antonio Llobet who neasured and studied the site. The positions of the flying object for each photograph are shown on the diagram as well as the original negative image area for each picture. Negatives X-1 and X-2 were snapped by Antonio Pardo from point A on the chart. Pardo forwarded two prints anonymously and though he said he took more he never re-established contact with the investigators. Negatives Y-1 through Y-5 were among those left at a photo developing shop for Antonio San Antonio by

22

another anonymous doner who seems to have taken more in his photo series also. The second set of pictures were snapped from point B in the diagram. Other witnesses among the picnickers at the scene reported seeing two male photographers in approximately those positions as they snapped pictures of the event. There is no evidence that the two photographers were acquainted with each other.

Negative Y-1 shows the ship in an edge-on view very similar to in X-2 except that at the moment of Y-1 one may see a corona discharge around the point where the cupola joins the upper disc surface. An enlargement of this image reveals the glow quite well. Please notice that there is no evidence of suspension in the enlarged picture. The object was rocking from side to side as it approached.

Picture Y-2 shows the first picture of the object tilted sharply up on edge in an exaggerated phase of the rocking motion, clearly revealing a symbol on the bottom of the ship.

Image Y-3 shows the object just after passing in its nearest approach to the photographers, and in Y-4 it is tilted at a steep angle again, once more revealing the symbol on the bottom. It may be seen in these pictures that the surface finish of the spacecraft does not look exactly like metals familiar to us. It has a more ceramic look and it was reported as being whitish in color as viewed from the picnick area. A fine glassy finish was also used to describe it.

Y-4 is one of the images analyzed by GSW in which they claim to have found a suspension line. Nobody else has been able to verify this. A considerable enlargement from the negatives still showed no evidence of any suspension.

A whole book was written about this case alone in the Spanish language only, UN CASO PERFECTO (ONE PERFECT CASE) by Antonio Ribera and Rafael Farriols, in which they describe their investigations in detail and what they found that convinced them of its validity. There is additional supporting evidence that fills seven full books on this case.

Identical UFOs have been photographed at least three other times elsewhere around the world and 350' of high grade 35mm movie film was shot with a theodolite camera

23

of an identical object over Andros Island off the coast of Florida on 21 May 1966.

Unknown to the photographers, or the spectators at the picnic ground, a group of men and women who had been in contact with the operators of this craft for some time (about 30 of them) had gathered at a small restaurant a few kilometers away as a result of identical messages posted individually to three of them, including Fernando Sesma Manzano, Alicia Araujo and Enrique Villagrasa, advising them in advance of the approximate place and time of the expected pick-up of some of their own expeditionary people there who had been in contact with these Spaniards. This is fully reported in UFO CONTACT FROM PLANET UMMO, Vol. I, The Mystery of UMMO, the English language version of EL MISTERIO DE UMMO by Antonio Ribera.

The craft left rectangular tripod landing marks on the ground at the landing site, and several metal artifacts of small size were later found at the place of the landing. The landing tracks were photographed, measured and tested for radiation and compaction.

The photographs analyzed by GSW were several lens systems away from the originals, being neither original negatives nor prints directly from the originals, being copies of copies as we can best determine at this time.

The very images published with the report should have negated the conclusions even if nothing were known of the inconclusive nature of the testing carried out by GSW. Our measurements upon the published computer image of the San Jose de Valderas photo used in this instance shows the width of the "suspension line" in this photo to be about 1.5 mm while the measured diameter of the whole ship in the same image with the same scale is 50 mm, only 33 times the width of the "line"! If everything were increased by a multiple of 10, the object would be 500 mm or about 20" in diameter and the line would now be 15mm or about the size of a 5/8" rope for a 20" model, an absurdity beyond imagining if a hoax were in fact intended.

An object 500 mm in diameter filling 16% of the photo image frame (measured in a full frame print) would have to be within 15 feet of the camera to produce that size combination. The infinity setting for such a camera is about 30 feet, so this would require a mid-range camera

24

setting for that shot. The time was late in the day so a wider diaphragm aparture was needed making the focus setting much more critical. A smaller object would have to be closer to the camera further complicating the problem. Under these conditions if the object were in focus (which it is) then the background would have to be considerably out of focus. If the background were in focus, this hypothetical model simply could not be at the same time.

If the object were larger, say 1,000mm (twice as big) then the "suspension line" would be an umbelievable 1¼" in diameter to suspend this 1 meter model.

French resarch scientists using better equipment than GSW failed to find any suspension line. We believe the evidence for validity of this series of photographs far outweighs the real contrary evidence produced up to now in this case.

Antonio Ribera

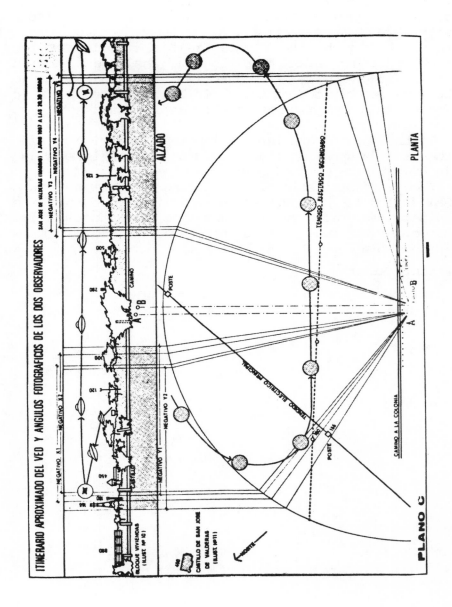

1 June 1967, San Jose de Valderas. Diagram of photo site from which Antonio Pardo and Antonio San Antonio's pictures were both taken of the same UFO at the same time.. Layout by Antonio Llobet.

i June 1967, 20:00, San Jose de Valderas, Spain, Photos X-1 and X-2
snapped by Antonio Pardo from location A on the diagram of the site
by Architect Antonio Llobet. Note the castle in the background.

27

1 June 1967, 20:00, San Jose de Valderas, Spain. Photos Y-1 and Y-2 in the hands of Antonio San Antonio, snapped from location B on the diagram of the site using a different camera with more telephoto magnification in the lens system.

28

1 June 1967, 20:00, San Jose de Valderas, Spain Photos Y-3 and Y-4 in the hands of Antonio San Antonio. Y-4 is one of the images tested by Ground Saucer Watch. Note the ceramic-like look to the finish.

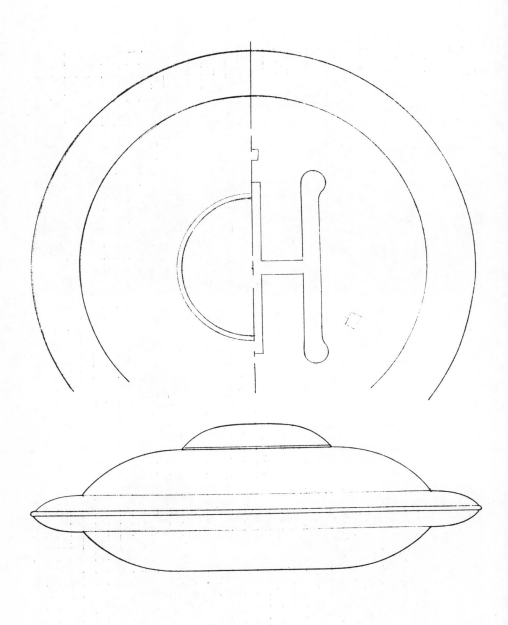

1 June 1967, 20:00, San Jose de Valderas. Enlargements of photos Nos. Y-1 and Y-1 delivered to Antonio San Antonio. These are two of the images analyzed by GSW. Observe carefully the lack of suspension, and the sharp straight lines making up the symbol vs computer inages.

MICROSCOPIC ANALYSIS
OF UFO PHOTOGRAPHS

There are some very specific steps in UFO photo analysis that can be most economically accomplished with good microscopes. For these examinations we should have a microscope with a camera adapter because it is here that we are most likely to detect one or another of the special effects techniques that can be employed to fake UFO photographs.

If we have the original negative or positive print, as the case may be, there are some specific tests possible that are not as productive on subsequent image generations.

Setting up the equipment and camera, we will carefully examine the following minimum points. We should look at these six points in at least 100x and 500x magnifications and some lower scales:

1. Read separately on the object image and again from the surrounding areas:
   a. A light colored area.
   b. A dark colored area.
   c. A grey or intermediate density area.
2. Read across the edge outlines of the object image in the photograph.
   a. The top edge.
   b. The bottom edge.
   c. Both side edges.

Having made a preliminary examination and come to some tentative conclusions we organize the next steps to concentrate on anything that seems to be of interest in making a complete evaluation. We will make the following minimum observations and be prepared to photograph through the microscope, anything that may be detected. We want to look for the following signals:

1. Areas too light indicating double exposure.
2. Areas too dark indicating overlay or lamination.
3. Composite grain pattern indicating re-photographing
4. Dust or dirt specks photographed indicating a copy.
5. Edges of image object too sharp or too fuzzy with reference to other objects in the picture. This may be

31

clues to airbrush, crayon or paste-up montage.

6. Comparative widths of edges around the object image in the picture. Is one edge wider, sharper, or fuzzier than the one on the opposite side?

Here we look carefully for homogenuity of silver nitrate grain particles and an even pattern of distribution in the emulsion, more easily seen in black and white pictures, and match it with the pattern of distribution for that batch number in the manufacturer's catalog. A re-exposure of any part of the image area with a different or another light source, or from a different angle, will activate more and different silver nitrate grains in the re-exposed area, and the change in appearance of the grain field is evident.

For color negatives or prints, we look for similar effects on the color granules and the crystals that make them up in the color layers.

We look at the several edges of the object image comparatively for sharpness, width of edge, and comparison with the edges of other objects in the picture. we look again for microscopic dirt and debris as evidence that we do not have in fact the original image.

We look for smearing and smudges in the lighter and the darker areas as evidence of reflected image or overlay which may result if the transparent medium is not clean enough

We look for evidence of suspension of a model which may not show up on any subsequent generation of the UFO photograph.

Prints from the slow-burn negatives made with smller diaphragm openings and longer exposure times should be made the same slow-burn way. Fainter details in the lighter areas are enhanced by this method while at the same time some detail in the denser areas may be lost. A reverse process with less exposure time will bring out detail in the denser areas but lose it in the lighter ones.

Light scatter analysis will reveal any objects in the picture which may be abnormally close to the camera such as a small object close-up. With moisture or haze it may be possible to measure the relative amounts of "distance greying" to the object image and compare it to

other objects in the picture to ascertain relative distances with respect to various other objects available.

In some photographs it may be possible to apply
more of these factors than in others, but in any case
all of the special effects techniques are detectable and
it is very difficult to get a hoax past all of the analysis techniques suggested here.

Additional photographic analysis techniques are
afforded us in the high technology sciences using lasers
and computers.

LASEROGRAPHIC ANALYSIS
OF UFO PHOTOGRAPHS

There are certain things in analysis of photographs
of UFOs that can be best studied through applications of
laser technology. With lasers we can scan film or transparencies in almost any scale we choose. This is something like working with a microscope except that we scan
with a coherent beam of light through the film negative
or positive transparency and analyse the resultant projection in extremely fine detail.

We examine the image medium, the transparent positive or negative film, and make preliminary judgements
about factors. Laser technology makes it possible for a
skilled examiner to determine much before he goes to a
computer. He can set up a grid, up to 10,000 lines per
centimeter horizontal and vertical, and go back and
forth scanning the whole picture. With the laserscope we
can blow this up in projection to any size we want, to
look at patterns and color laminations. We can even look
at individual silver nitrate grains and color granules
in the film emulsion and make judgements particle by
particle.

With laser holography techniques we can create a
3-dimensional image from a 2-dimensional flat photograph
and laser projection of the hologram is so fine that a
tenth of a centimeter square can be blown up to many
feet if desired to view the emulsion condition in 3-D.
Homogenuity of the silver grains and color granules can
be studied for deviation from norm caused by selective
re-exposure or by aberrent light.

With a computer we can isolate the different planes
of focus, or planes of blurring within the image field,
even when all the objects in the picture are beyond the
fixed infinity, or true focus point, of the lens system
used.

Using the laser we make holographic plates where we
go first to the extreme depth-of-field, to the horizon,
where we run verticals to get some idea of the true
focus there. Then we work back through closer points to
the main focus field and designate that. In the same way

we will find the nearest focus plane, inside the focal-point setting used for the picture, if such objects appear in the picture, and designate that.

Then we will work inside these limits, setting up as many additional focus planes as we have objects in the image frame to tie them to. We will make a laser holographic plate for each of these designated planes by isolating, with a video-laser technique, things that have a particular amount of blur. Then we will set up programs to judge why an object image is blurred. Is it because it is out of focus or because it is moving, or because the camera is moving? Or is it because it is vibrating in a field, or because a field is vibrating around it? The boundary lines of things will tell us what the focus at that point is. An index is designated for this in single or double digit algorythems. In digital analysis we can draw certain conclusions about how distant things are by how sharp the real focus is. This is observed and registered as blur factor. By going to the object most in focus and then deciding where the true depth of field really lies, we can determine the depth of field of each point in the picture with relation to other points. We can then set up holographic plates for each depth of field identified in the photograph and give them sequential order. We can now call them up in serial from front to back, or back to front, as we choose and then rotate the array to either side, say 30 degrees, and see all the planes in 3-dimensional relationship. Now we can tell what is in front of or behind anything else in the picture.

This whole process is based on the reality that the picture field in not really all in focus from the infinity setting to the horizon. It only appears so to our untrained eye because the amount of apparent change in focus is so small beyond the farthest distance setting of the camera.

Of course we we can repeat many steps with the laserscope that we could already have done with a microscope although the applications are different and one serves to confirm the other.

We can transfer the image, by laser projection through the film transparency or negative, to a charged coupled plate and introduce the image data into the computer memory system even grain by grain of the silver nitrate crystals that make up a black and white picture for exmple. Or we can fill the video image screen with a single color granule if that becomes important. In one of the distance measurement techniques this does assume importance. Such fidelity is more difficult with hard copy prints. It is impossible with other than originals.

With laserography techniques we can analyse area by area the blurring, color scale, grey scale, image density, light scatter, and any other variable in the picture.

FLYING CYLINDERS

Among the earliest known photographs of Unidentified Flying Objects is one of a cylinder-shaped craft made on 11 April 1897 at Rogers Park, a few miles north of Chicago, by Walter Mc Cann together with three other witnesses, G. A. Oversucker, William Needles and E. L. Osborne. The object flew over the city quite low in the early morning sky and was photographed above the skyline with one of the early cameras which was quite primitive by todays standards. A sketch of that photograph was published in the Chicago Tribune along with a remark that the photograph had been examined by experts and was pronounced genuine. Robert Emenegger reproduced a copy of this sketch from the newspaper in his book, UFOs PAST, PRESENT AND FUTURE.

Other cylinder-shaped craft were seen in the sky in the late 1890s but so far as is known, very few other photographs of them were made. A similar object was reportedly photographed over Grand Rapids, Michigan less than an hour later, but we have been unable to discover copies of the pictures or any eyewitnesses to the photo prints. On 26 April 1897, at Baring Cross, Mr. C. D. Lawrence reportedly photographed a broadside view of a cylindrical airship about 40 feet long and pointed at both ends. The same, or a very similar photograph, was reported to have been made at Little Rock, Arkansas at about the same time by a Mr. G. L. We suspect that this is the same photograph with its identification confused by an error in reporting. Another airship was allegedly photographed in Chile on 27 July 1897 but no details are available. Mr. Lucius Farish, an avid student of the earliest UFO cases, has a record of an airship photographed over New Mexico in 1901.

Leonard Stringfield reported a case revealed to him by a Mr. C.J.J. (true identity known to Mr Stringfield), of a massive wingless cylindrical craft that appeared quite suddenly behind a U.S. Bomber over the Bay of Biscay in November 1942. This occurred off the west French coast in broad daylight. The bomber was on an anti-submarine patrol when the object overtook it and flew alongside for 15 minutes. Sgt. F.M.S. snapped a number of photographs with a Fairchild K-20 aerial camera which makes an 8" by 10" negative. Then the object gained altitude, made a 180 degree turn and sped away. Only one photograph of the lot -- the one made with a filter -- turned out, and in C.J.J.'s words was, "a perfect print". U.S. Intelligence has never released any of the pictures or any information on this case.

Several years later, in 1945 and 1946, several photographs of, then called "Ghost Rockets", that were being reported in increasing numbers over Scandinavia, were published in the London Daily Telegraph. Mr Eric Reuterswaard snapped a picture on 16 August 1946 of a comet-like object in the sky above the islands just outside of Stockholm. With super-sensitive processing, performed at the request of the Swedish General Staff, a cylindrical object was found in the midst of the "flame". The U.S. Navy photographed an identical object over Sweden during "Operation Mainbrace" in September 1952.

Three years later, on 23 February 1949, Commander A.V. Orrego shot 8mm movie footage of a huge luminous cylindrical object that maneuvered about over the Chilean Antarctic Base. Base personnel also shot still pictures with hand cameras of this glowing cigar that changed position and elevation and even attitude of flight, at times being seen lying horizontally in the air and at other times seen standing on end vertically or tilted at an angle to the horizon. This object was seen at various times for three days in both daylight and dark although it was light most of the day at this time of year. In daylight it was also seen as a shiny silvery object that occasionally launched and recovered smaller objects that flew around independently while they were outside the larger vehicle. Radio contact was established with the Argentine and American Missions nearby on the Antarctic Continent and they reported similar observations and that they too had made photographs.

Commander Orrego also maintained close contact with his government in Santiago and as soon as the activity ended he was picked up and rushed home with the mission film. The newspapers had gotten wind of the sensational story and besieged the government for information. Several photographs and a story were released to the city newspapers and they all carried front page spreads with pictures at that time. Then the information on what was being done about the pictures and the story details was closed and nothing more was heard about the case. For some reason it seemed to have been shrouded in secrecy.

An interesting sidelight developed on this particular case in 1982 when we were approached by a Chilean Col. in their Intelligence, now living in exile in another country, who wanted us to make representations to our government for return of the Chilean Intelligence files on UFO activity, including the Borrego report, which were trucked away by U.S. Intelligence agents in the midst of the overthrow and murder of President Allende the very night that he was being killed! This raises all kinds of questions that we do not have answers to and so we only offer this much information for what it is worth to any who have a better opportunity to do something about it. Remember, this flap took place in 1949 outside of our country, and we did not hear about it publicly for years.

Back in the United States, on 5 March 1951, at about 10:30 PM, Mr. George Adamski of Palomar Terraces, California, after 5 years of fleeting glimpses of strange flying craft through his 6 inch Newtonian style telescope, and occasional snapshots of luminous objects with his camera rigged to the eyepiece, succeeded in taking 5 pictures of a cigar-shaped craft that he had seen before but was unable to photograph. Not only did he photograph it this time, he was actually able to take a series of 5 pictures of the large craft in the act of launching smaller luminous, circular, domed, disc-shaped craft that emerged from the belly of the mother-ship and flew around the larger craft.

There are a lot of strange things that happen in this business of UFO investigation, but among the most disconcerting is the amount of unnecessary blunder in dealing with the phenomena. Too frequently good evidence is "lost" or "stolen", removed from the mail, damaged in processing or handling, etc., and this case is no exception. Those pictures of the mother-ship launching the smaller craft that were released did not show all there was to see. The little luminous objects are not just blobs of light as they were printed. They were in fact domed discs with a row of small bright lights around the rim. When the picture was overexposed in developing to reveal the dim outline of the dark ship, the small luminous objects "flared our" with too much light and the

39

detail was lost. Mr. C.A. Honey had the original negatives locked up which clearly showed the detail of the
smaller objects and only a few prints were ever made and
none were published.

Over a year and a half later, on 13 December 1952, he
succeeded in photographing one of these smaller versions
of the variety of craft carried by the mother-ship, in
close-up view through this same telescope.

An interesting characteristic of this zeppelin-shaped
ship was the very blunt front and rear ends, a characteristic that would show up later in photographs of this
type of larger ship.

A strange and unexpected corroboration of the Adamski
sighting and photographs came about in the following
manner: Mr. Ray Fetterman, a route salesman in the south
Claifornia area, and his wife Helen were visiting some
friends living in Cajon Canyon, and Ray and his friend
were standing in the back yard drinking a refreshment
that forenoon, when a glint of light in the sky caught
their attention. Looking up, Ray said he saw a huge dark
cigar-shaped craft hanging motionless in the sky above,
and around it were moving 2 then 3 brightly luminous
dots. As they watched, they observed the larger ship
give birth to two more of the smaller objects, which all
seemed to emerge from the central belly of the large dark
cylindrical shape, and the whole spectacle gradually
drifted away and out of sight. He called Helen to come
out and see it before it was gone. The time was reconstructed to be a forenoon on a Monday in early March of
1951, as best they could remember, having made no notes
at the time. This comes close to the time of Mr. Adamski's observation and photographs. The Fettermans however, had never heard of Adamski and had never heard of
or seen the book published later which contained those
Adamski photographs, nor had they ever seen copies of
them anywhere else. They were in fact unaware that any
such pictures existed at the time that Ray told me this
story.

But unknown to Mr. Adamski or Ray Fetterman, less than
a month earlier, on 19 February 1951, at 07:20 AM,
passengers M. Bicknell and a friend with him shot 8mm
motion picture footage from their Loadstar airliner in
flight, of a huge cigar-shaped craft flying over Mount

Kilimanjaro in Kenya, East Africa. The shape of this cigar-shaped vessel was identical with that photographed by Adamski and described by Ray Fetterman.

Then on the 8th and 9th of January 1956 (seven years after the 23 February 1949 Borrego film), two very big cylindrical UFOs were photographed together in the south polar skies, a most rare occurrance. A Chilean government scientific team on Robertson Island in the Weddell Sea of Chilean Antarctica observed them all day for two days and took many still photographs and movies in both black and white and color. The two huge craft, estimated to be about 460 feet long by 80 feet in diameter, hung in a vertical position in the sky at first, but they changed position and attitude a number of times. They moved fast and slow, changed positions, made sharp angled turns in direction, and changed colors as they maneuvered about. Then they resumed vertical position again. They were estimated to carry out most of these operations at near the 30,000 foot level although they did come down lower several times.

Observations were made with binoculars and other viewing and photographic devices including movie and still cameras. Radio contact was established with the Argentine and American missions again and they called relative positions back and forth and worked triangulation problems to calculate altitudes and speeds. Again the mission team chief was flown home with the evidence and once more a limited release was made to the local newspapers and made the front pages. That was all that was released publicly as before. The intelligence officer provided the first information we had about the second Antarctica spectacular when he indicated that those film and report documents were in the files carried away the night of the asassaination of Allende.

Personal appeal from a Chilean Intelligence Officer

On 15 March 1956, many photographs were taken of a big cylindrical UFO that maneuvered about over the city of Salta, Argentina.

On 23 March 1956, Astronomer Roberto Ozorno of Mexico photographed a large cylinder-shaped UFO over Mexico City. This object had abruptly squared ends, very similar to the Adamski pictures but perhaps a little more slenderness for length in proportion.

Eleven years later, during the great UFO Flap of 1967, on 3 July 1967, Mr. Joseph L. Ferriere, a chemist for a textile plant, was walking in a scrub area near Cumberland, Rhode Island, that had power lines running through it and a water reservoir nearby. It was between 19:15 and 19:30 in the afternoon when he turned to look back over his left shoulder behind him, "And there was this fantastic object just hanging in the sky," he said.

"It was cylinder shaped and moving very slowly, just sort of rocking, the way a boat rocks on the water. I grabbed my camera and took two or three photographs as the craft began to move to my right. I noticed an opening in the bottom of the ship, at least it looked like an opening. Suddenly I saw something slip out of the opening very fast, like it was ejected or catapulted. This object went away from the mother-ship. For a moment I was rattled and didn't know which object to focus my camera on. I decided to stick with the larger craft and got another picture of it. Suddenly, without any sound it changed to a vertical position, in a flash of a second, and took off straight up! It just took-off. I almost missed it, but I did manage to get a shot of it as it was disappearing at great speed."

"I then concentrated on the smaller saucer-type craft that had slipped out of the belly of the mother-ship, and managed to get a couple shots of this craft with its domed disc-shape; one as it approached toward overhead, and another as it took-off in the direction where I had first deen the mother-ship."

Mr. Farriere said that his first impression of the big mother-craft was that it was about 200 to 250 feet long. Later he decided that it could have been as small as 150 feet long. Since he had no reference point in the sky with which to compare the object, actual size is all a matter of gursswork. He was disbelieved and intimidated over the story and may have revised his guess downward in defense of the reality of the sighting. We believe the original estimate to be the more accurate, and more in conformance with the size of this type reported elsewhere.

He estimated the small disc-shaped craft to be about 12 feet or so in diameter, but again noted that he had no accurate way to measure the size to any degree of accuracy.

42

Mr Ferriere reported that while observing the mother-ship, he noticed something that appeared to be "plunging in and out" of what he called the rear of the long ship. It was moving in and out very slowly in a quite regular sequence. He said the mother-ship was colored a very drab, unreflecting charcoal gray, with four lighter circular "spots" along the side. He said the spots didn't appear to be glass or plastic. He estimated that he observed the craft for three or four minutes while it was launching its saucer-shaped small craft, and then it flipped up on end and raced up into the heavens. There was no noise, not even when it took off. "There was not one bit of noise," said Ferriere, "It just flipped up vertically, no rocking or anything, and in a matter of seconds it was out of sight."

These photographs were offered to Dr. J. Allen Hynek and the Condon Committee for examination and analysis, but nothing to Ferriere's knowledge was done to study them. These photographs were examined extensively by August C. Roberts, an expert in photo technology, who said there was no evidence of photo trickery of fraud. Roberts said, "I have known Mr. Ferriere for a number of years, and his character, honesty and integrity are beyond question. Time will prove the truth of this experience."

Bachelor News, Vol. 2, No. 9, Saturday 30 March 1968

But that was not the end of that story. Within 3 weeks of publishing that report a man came up from Washington (D.C.) and bought out Bachelor News, put out two more issues and closed the weekly paper down forever. So Joe Ferriere, now a confirmed UFO believer, established his own magazine, PROBE, to publish UFO case material for interested students of the phenomenon. His premier issue featured his own photographs and the story of the sighting and photographic event. He set up a second UFO photographic story for his second issue and had a third one in the works when a man from Washington bought out the magazine and the rights and closed it down forever.

Joe Ferriere was harassed, threatened and abused. He was followed and he felt sure his phone was tapped. His mail was being tampered with and strange problems developed in his life. A time came when he told August Roberts he wished he had never photographed the thing or told the story. He said he had even considered denying the whole experience and letting people think it was a hoax if it would get rid of his problems. He suggested Roberts declare it a fake or find some way to take the "heat" off, as it was seriously interferring with his life.

On 6 May 1972, near Sugaru City, Aomori Prefecture, Japan, the sister of Kenji Ogala snapped a photograph of a distant mountain scene showing a cigarette-shaped cylindrical object in the sky in the background. The object was registered in the film as a photographed image and its distance was confirmed by atmospheric graying visible between the object and the lens. Kenji found the picture in her album and sent it to a Japanese UFO magazine for analysis. He did not ask his sister about the picture because he did not want her to know that he had been going through her album. She had never mentioned the picture in his presence.

On 20 January 1974, Shigaru Wakamatsu, 23 years old, was riding a train in Europe between Rome and Geneve, when about noon, he spotted a strange cylinder-shaped object flying high in the sky. He got out his camera and snapped one photograph of it before it was gone.

Near the end of January 1974, Hideo Takagi, eighteen years old, from his home in the Katsushika District of Saitama Prefecture, Japan, took 5 pictures of a Japanese blimp flying overhead. When he got them back from the developer, he saw that in two of them a dark cylinder-shaped object, very much higher and farther away, was clearly captured on film. Atmospheric graying due to the distance between the lens and the object was clearly visible in the object imaged in the film emulsion.

Mrs. Mitsuko Yasuzuka, a 40 year old teacher from Iwabune, Japan, was walking on Yaizu Beach on 6 May 1974, and decided to photograph a large black rock that rose out of the surf there. It was about 07:40 AM as she made two pictures of the scene. When the developed prints came back from the processor, she was surprised to see that she had also captured a huge cylinder-shaped dark object flying very high in the distant sky. The second photograph made only a few seconds later showed the same dark cylinder-shaped object many more miles distant and closer to the horizon over the sea. Photographic experts who examined the negatives ruled out the possibility of a film flaw or developing defect and declared that a real object was photographed at a great distance.

On 23 July 1974, at about 13:00, from Miura Peninsula, Japan, Masao Yamanaka, 26 years old, took a picture of ships in the water off the cape. In the developed prints he discovered a dark cylinder-shaped object in the distant sky. He did not see it when the picture was made.

On the 26th of July 1974, again over Japan, at Lake Onogawa, near Tokyo, high school student Masahiko Sugio, with his Petri V-6 camera, saw and photographed a similar huge cylinder-shaped object high in the sky over the quiet lake and some hills.

Only 3 days later, on 29 July 1974, at about 10:00 AM, high school student Takayuki Hanawa photographed at a place near Kirigamine, Nagano Prefecture, Japan, a dark cylinder-shaped UFO over a beautiful green field near the winter ski resort. He was taking a picture of the quietly beautiful scene in its summer garb. In this particular case a dark spherical object, aparently launched by the larger craft, was also captured in the same photograph. Hanawa did not notice either object at the time he was taking the picture. Photographic experts declared that this was not a film flaw or a defect in processing, but a real object photographed at a distance.

Almost one year later, at Nagoya City, Nagoya Prefecture, on 3 September 1975, at 14:30 in the afternoon, young Hirohito Tanaka, 12 years old, from the verhadah of his home, saw and photographed a dark gray cylinder-shaped craft of immense size flying in the sky above. He snapped 8 black and white photographs with his economical hand camera as the machine launched three small dark round-looking objects, which then flew independently around the mother-ship. They all drifted away and out of sight together. Some of the small craft descended and made low passes over the city but did not land. Young Hirohito's mother and brother watched as he photographed the unusual spectacle.

45

This was almost a repeat of the early Adamski night photograohs except this was observed in full daylight, was photographed without a telescope, and was filmed in front of witnesses. Here again the typical blunt ended cylindrical form that Mr. Adamski originally photographed shows up. There is no doubt of the distance from the camera in this case because the distance graying of the haze of the city is clearly evident. It was later learned that this same young man and some of his friends also witnessed a similar performance on an earlier occasion near his home in Nagoya. In that event the cigar-shaped mother-ship was preceeded by a flight of several round objects of smaller size that flew rapidly to and fro in the sky above them.

The last eight cases are from the files of KOZUMO, a slick Japanese UFO Journal published in Tokyo

Considering the amount of evidence here and the lack of communication between the various witnesses involved it is difficult to discount them all and say that this type of phenomena does not exist. We must also remember that this is only a skimming of what may be available. This is only from such cases **reported** while it is usually conceded that for every case reported there may be as many as ten more unreported.

Nor can we discount them all as hoaxes and pretend they didn't happen at all. We had two more cases of this type of UFO photographed that we have held back because of unanswered questions that leave them in some doubt. The photographs could easily be distinguished from the rest of the cases reported here and so we have pulled them out of this report.

FLYING CYLINDERS

 5 Mar 1951, 22:30, Palomar Terraces, George Adamski

 3 Jul 1967, 19:15, Cumberland, Rhode Island, Ferriere

   Jan 1974,   Saitama Prefec. Japan, Hideo Takagi

 6 May 1974, 07:40, Yaizu Beach, Japan, Mitsuko Yasuzuka

29 Jul 1974, 10:00, Kirigamine, Nagano, Jap., T. Hanawa

 3 Sep 1975, 14:30, Nagoya City, Japan, Hirohito Tanaka

PALOMAR TERRACES, CALIFORNIA
5 March 1951, 22:30

On 5 March 1951, after five years of fleeting glimpses of unusual and unidentified flying objects seen through his 6 inch Newtonian style telescope, Mr. George Adamski succeeded in photographing the "big one" that he had observed before. He had rigged a home-made camera attachment to the eyepiece of his telescope and had been able to photograph some of the strange glowing flying objects earlier with moderate success, and had been advised by his intelligence contacts to try to get a picture of the big one which may be the source of the smaller craft already seen and photographed. At night the smaller objects glowed with a yellow-orange luminosity and in daylight they looked silvery metallic and reflective.

But at about 22:30 this night of 5 March, he was looking through his telescope and picked up the big cylinder shape again. This cylinder was not exactly cylindrical but was a straight cylinder in the middle, then slightly tapering sections for the last third on each end, terminating in ends that seemed to be cut off almost square but at a slight angle.

As he watched, a bright glow appeared on the belly of the dark shape he was observing, and he snapped a photo of that. It separated and slowly rose above the level of the larger craft as another one began to emerge. He shot a picture of that one also, getting both the mother-ship and the two smaller glowing objects in the frame. Then a third and a fourth and fifth emerged the same way and he succeeded in getting photographs of them each time, taking 5 pictures in all.

The smaller craft which emerged from the bottom side of the dark cigar-shape were not a single yellow-white light, but a row of small brilliant lights in a horizontal ilne as though they were positioned around the edge of a disc. When the photo prints were over-contrasted as well as over-printed to bring out the dark cigar shape in the dark sky, the row of lights on the smaller ships flared out into the appearance of a bar of light, giving in fact a false appearance.

Unknown to Adamski, on the following morning, the 6th of March, Mr. Ray Fetterman, a route salesman in that

48

southern part of California, and his wife Helen, were visiting friends living in Cajone Canyon, about 60 miles NNE of Palomar, and Ray and his friend were standing in the back yard of the residence, drinking a refreshment when a glint in the sky caught their attention. Looking up, Ray said he saw a huge gray cigar-shaped craft, like a zeppelin, hanging motionless in the sky above them, and around it were moving 2 or 3 brilliantly luminous dots of light. As they stood there and watched, they saw the larger craft "give birth" to two more of the smaller objects, which seemed to emerge from the central belly of the larger ship. The sholw spectacle gradually drifted away and out of sight. They did call the women out to see the show before it was gone. They had never heard of Adamski and in fact were unaware that any such photos existed at the time that I first interviewed them.

There were other witnesses to this same or a similar cigar-shaped mother-ship also. On 20 November 1952, Mr. Adamski, accompanied by Mrs. Alice K. Wells, the owner of Palomar Gardens and Mrs. Lucy McKinnis, together with Mr. and Mrs. Al C. Bailey and Dr. and Mrs. George Hunt Williamson, proceeded to a point north of Desert Center, California, indicated to both parties as a possible spot for a meeting with an entity they were independently in some kind of telepathic contact with, and this meeting had been suggested by the entity, and they were responding to an arrangement made.

At about 11:00 they were all parked, both cars, beside the road some 11 miles north of Desert Center. As George Adamski and Al Bailey explored the surrounding area, the women prepared a picnic lunch they had brought for this purpose. They had all watched a twin-engined airplane pass over in the clear blue sky above, when their attention was suddenly drawn back to the closest mountain ridge which the plane had crossed just moments before. "Riding high and without a sound, there was a gigantic cigar-shaped silvery ship, without wings or appendages of any kind. Slowly, almost as if it were drifting, it came in our direction; then seemed to stop, hovering motionless." Adamski and Al Bailey jumped in one car with Lucy driving and raced about a half mile along the hiway, then turned off on a trail in towards the ridge and stopped about a half mile in, to the west of the highway where Adamski got out telling the others to go back with the rest and watch. The whole time this was going on the huge ship had slowly followed the car and was then about directly overhead. While Lucy and Al were returning in the car the huge flying machine turned in the sky and silently crossed over the top of the mountain ridge and was lost from sight just before a number of military airplanes arrived overhead. Adamski set up his telescope and camera attachment, hoping all the time that the big ship would return after the airplanes left the area...

When he turned around the stranger from the telepathic source was standing there and a small ship was parked a short distance away. That was Adamski's famous first meeting with his communicator. While the equipment was not set up in time, and no pictures of the spacecraft were made, there were six witnesses to the overhead pass of the cigar-shaped craft, and they agreed that it was the same as the one photographed through the telescope on 5 March 1951

It was only 2 weeks before Adamski's photographs of 5 March at Palomar that passengers M. Bicknell and friend shot motion pictures of a very similar cylindrical gray metallic object from an airliner in flight. At 07:20 AM on 19 February 1951 the two passengers were riding on a Loadstar airliner flying over Mount Kilimanjaro in Kenya of East Africa, when they spotted the huge cigar-shaped craft also flying above the mountain. It was cylindrical in the middle, tapering slightly in the last third of its length toward each end which terminated in an abrupt cut-off at a slight angle.

Adamski could not have known of these movies before he shot the night launch sequence because the roll of movie film had not been developed yet, and Bicknell could not have known that Adamski would photograph the same kind of ship in a few days. Neither of them ever heard of Ray Fetterman and he knew nothing of either of these photographers or events.

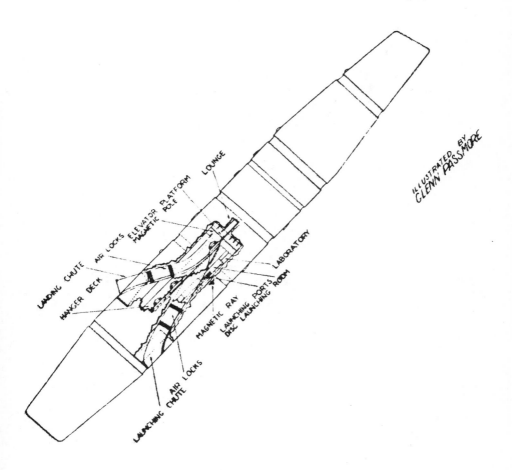

Illustrated by Glenn Passmore

Labels: LANDING CHUTE, AIR LOCKS, ELEVATOR PLATFORM, MAGNETIC POLE, LOUNGE, HANGER DECK, MAGNETIC RAY, LAUNCHING PORTS, DISC LAUNCHING ROOM, LABORATORY, AIR LOCKS, LAUNCHING CHUTE

5 March 1961, 22:30, Palomar Terraces, California. This is a line drawing of the cylindrical mother-ship that Adamski photographed in the process of launching five smaller craft at night. This drawing was made by Glenn Passmore for INSIDE THE SPACESHIPS by Adamski. The drawing was constructed from Adamski's descriptions of the interior of the craft after being taken aboard. This was naturally rejected at the time because he happened to be one of the first. We have accounts of hundreds of such cases worldwide today.

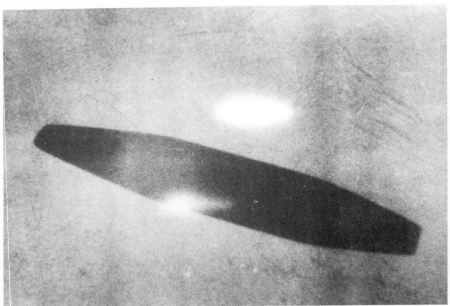

5 March 1961, 22:30, Palomar Terraces, California. As George Adamski
watches through his telescope he sees the first lighted shuttle craft
emerge from the belly of the dark cylinder and snaps the first photo,
using his home-made camera adapter on the eyepiece of the telescope.

5 March 1961, 22:30, Palomar Terraces, California. Adamski has seen five smaller craft emerge and has photographed them. Note that what appears to be bars of light are actually rows of small round lights around the rim of the smaller craft. They all came from the belly of the larger ship and went back in at the top.

CUMBERLAND, RHODE ISLAND
3 July 1967, 19:15

Joseph L. Ferriere had been working part-time with a radio station in Woonsocket, R.I. at the time, and was then working as an announcer. He was also a local UFO investigator and had interviewed a number of people on strange events and phenomenon in the vicinity. For two or three days, he had been receiving telephone calls at the station from people asking him if he knew anything at all about a large dirigible-like object being seen flying about over the east Woonsocket area. It was down the road toward Cumberland from where the radio station was located. According to Ferriere:

"This went on for a couple of days. I used to get a lot of calls -- from doing the radio shows, and I'm not gonna go running down every- everybody who calls in to report something funny in the sky. But after a couple of days, and everybody seemed to be pinpointing pretty much of a closely confined geographical area, I said, 'What the hell, something is going on in this area, I'll give it a shot.' I bought me a camera. It was a $9.00 camera, and a box reflex."

"I thought I had the area pinpointed pretty well, and I wasn't surprised to find that power lines ran right through this area. So I went in under the power lines, and in off the road maybe a half mile, or a mile, and I started looking around... There was nothing there. And I started looking around for traces. I figured, well maybe there would be some physical traces, or evidence that something may have been through there. And I did that for maybe a half hour or so, or 45 minutes. I found nothing and I remember laughing to myself and saying, 'Well if you don't know what you are looking for, you could be looking right at the damn thing and you would-n't recognize it anyway, so this is stupid. Let's get out of here. There's nothing happening. You've checked it out, and that's it,' and I was about to leave, and as I turned around to leave I spotted a cigar-shaped thing in the sky."

"My inmediate impression was that this thing was any-where between 100' and 150' in length. And I took a picture of it as quickly as I could. And I was standing on a hill, almost at the top, and this (object) was maybe 75' to 100' above tree-top level. Very, very low. Absolutely no sound, and almost... because I was on a hill, it was almost on a direct eye level with me -- a little bit higher."

"And I experienced that kind of thing that you read about all the time. I was at first surprised to see the thing and my curiosity overcame the initial reaction, and I started acting very histerically. I've got the camera and I'm going to get as many shots as I can. I took 4 shots I think, 4 or 5 shots of the long cigar-shaped object. Incidentally, that looked to me, -I don't know if I can make you see this -- itlooked to me like it was made out of stone or rock -- it didn't look metallic. It looked like it had a rocky and uneven-like, charcoal-like surface. I took 4 pictures of it and I noticed what looked like a hatch on the bottom of the object. It was at a 45 degree angle, opened out and down."

"And on one end of the object, there was a piston-like device, pumping in and out. It was about one block, one city block, about 500 feet away, and that might be stretching it. It might have been a little closer, I don't know. But I saw that piston-like thing going in and out slowly, and the hatch-like affair on the bottom of it."

"After I took 4 or 5 shots of it, I did see movement. I saw something flash out of the bottom, out of that hatchway there. It was just a blurr of speed, something, and it caused my attention to be focussed away from the thing, and I looked -- and I looked off to my left and did see a smaller disc-shaped object just hanging there, and I just assumed that it came out of there (the open hatch in the ship). But something happened and so I got a couple of shots of that, and then the disc started moving away very, very rapidly. I think I had one shot (of film) left. I was confused at that point. I didn't know whether I should try to get another shot of the disc or another shot of the larger object, and I decided on the larger object because it was larger... So I went to take the last shot, of the cigar-shaped thing, and as I did so, it went from a horizontal - it flipped up, to a vertical position and started to move out of my line of vision. I snapped the picture anyway and (I) got just a piece of the object as it moved out of my line of vision (through the camera viewfinder)."

"I think the whole time might have taken -- the time gets all messed up -- it was definitely inside of five minutes, and maybe more like three. It seemed longer. Now, in retrospect, it seems like it might have taken 15 to 20 minutes, but I know that it didn't. It was within a five minute range anyway."

"I saw four lighter circular areas on the side of the thing (the cigar-shape), but they didn't look like windows. They just looked like four lighter areas -- just looked as though four lighter spots along-side were on the surface itself."

"The negatives are with ___ now. He is trying to make some better prints."

About the time of this interview August Roberts shot several rolls of film of Joe Ferriere and his pictures, as well as the photo site and other associated subjects. He sent them in for commercial developing through a local service, and "lost" the whole lot through a "mistake" in the processing lab and the film was replaced. This might be an acceptable excuse to one who is not aware of the unusually high frequency of such "losses", but in our experience such "losses" involving UFO subjects run manyfold higher than any other losses in photo processing.

But that was nothing compared to the hassels that followed Joe Ferriere after his experience with photographing UFOs. He had suddenly gone from investigator to one of "them", from critic to observer. Joe Ferriere had at least one outstanding characteristic that particularly suited him as a UFO investigator. He was objective and he was fair. He was also extremely honest and very intelligent. He was also motivated by truth above financial gain, something that can hardly be applied to most of the critics of this phenomenon.

Joe Farriere now had a new truth that He knew beyond all doubt to be literally true. He felt an acute urge to communicate his new discovery to others seeking the real answers. He had also been investigation another local UFO story, involving UFO photographs, and had even witnessed that observer take two photographs of the disc-shaped flying object. Now there were two positive cases that he had verified for himself, and he thought there must be others seeking the answers like himself. He finally decided to publish the two cases, and others from his files in a modest magazine format. He then prepared a spread and laid out the first issue of PROBE, an excellent private production. He somehow encountered a Mr. Morton J. Lewis, a promoter who wanted to distribute the new magazine for Ferriere. Lewis arranged to ship thousands of copies to magazine distributors, and when Ferriere verified their orders they checked out properly and he shipped, and paid Lewis his commissions on these sales. By the end of 45 days no payments had come in on the magazine sales, and Ferriere's creditors were losing patience. He began to ask the recipients for payment, and instead of paying they sent all the magazines back to Ferriere, many of the boxes still unopened, and Ferriere now had to pay for return shipment too. The new magazine venture had failed, and his creditors demanded payment of their accounts against him.

In this crisis situation Ferriere received a telephone call from Washington, from a Mr. Harold Salkin, who said he was associated with the Little Listening Post, a well known UFO study group, and he wanted to come up and discuss Ferriere's photographs. This was before the photos had been published anywhere, except in the failed Probe.

In an attempt to salvage something to pay his bills, Joe Ferriere had released a spread on these pictures to be published in Bachelor News, a New York Tabloid. They were eventually printed as a front page headline special by Bachelor News but this was only in work at this time.

Harold Salkin arrived with a thuggish-looking man by the name of Gordon. Salkin also wanted to distribute the new probe magazine, but the last distribution effort had cost so much that Ferriere was afraid of getting into another and explained the problem to Salkin. Salkin then asked how much Ferriere still owed, and Ferriere gave him a figure over $2,000.00. Salkin wrote Ferriere a check for $2,500.00 and arranged with Farriere to make up and publish a second issue of Probe, which Salkin would finance. He wanted no control, not even of distribution by this time, and suggested that a listing as co-producer would be adequate. Salkin and Gordon then left to go back to Washington.

About a week later a letter arrived from Salkin with another check for $2,500.00 to pay for the second issue of Probe, which Ferriere then prepared, featuring the Harold Trudel story and photographs, and published this one also.

Still not hearing from Salkin, Ferriere tried to contact him at the telephone number left, to tell him that the second issue was done and he was starting layout on a third issue. He could not reach Salkin at the telephone number, and when he had it traced, it turned out to be a hotel room.

So Ferriere then contacted Clair Young at The Little Listening Post, who was then editing their newsletter. Salkin had mentioned that he knew her, and apparently Harold Salkin did, but Clair Young told Ferriere that Harold Salkin was in a mental institution, and to the best of her knowledge he had been there for about 5 years! So Ferriere didn't say anything about his strange visitor and hung up. At that point he had had enough. He just wanted to quit. He had no idea who the imposter really was, and never saw him again. His bills were paid and he was even, and he was content to let the whole thing drop.

Bachelor News put out their special edition featuring these spectacular photographs and the story on the front page, and then went through about the same experience as Ferriere with the distribution – without a benefactor. The issues all came back unsold, even still in their shipping boxes like the Probe magazines. It bankrupted Bachelor News and they folded owing $12,000.00 for the printing bill.

Joe Ferriere snapped 7 photographs during that sighting event using his new Pho-Tak 620 Reflex No. 1, camera with a 14mm color corrected fixed-focus lens. It was made in Chicago. The film was Kodak black and white negative film of standard commercial grade at the time.

Unknown to Joe Ferriere, the following letter report existed in Australia: "Tuesday, November 15, 1960, Hampstead, N.W. 3: This morning at 8:30 a.m. I saw a mysterious object hovering above me -- it was cylindrical in shape, with a row of four or five windows on the side, fairly high, It appeared to be made of silver metal, extremely brilliant. It made a rapid course of about 45 to 60 degrees from the horizontal. It was eventually hidden by house-roofs. The visibility was excellent, the sky clear. The object traveled absolutely silent. I enclose a sketch of what I saw--."
David W.I.C. Vessey, 10 Uphill Grove, Mill Hill, N.W. 7.

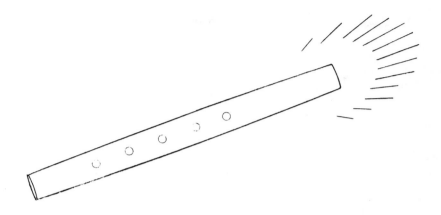

15 November 1960, 08:30, Hampstead, N.W., Australia. This sketch was made by David W.I.C. Vessey of the silent silvery metallic cylinder-shaped object he observed. Note the "windows" along the side.

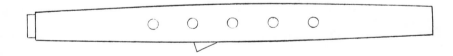

3 July 1967, 19:15, Cumberland, Rhode Island. Line drawing of the 100' to 150' long cigar-shaped mother-ship which apparently launched the smaller disc-shaped craft from the open hatch in the belly.

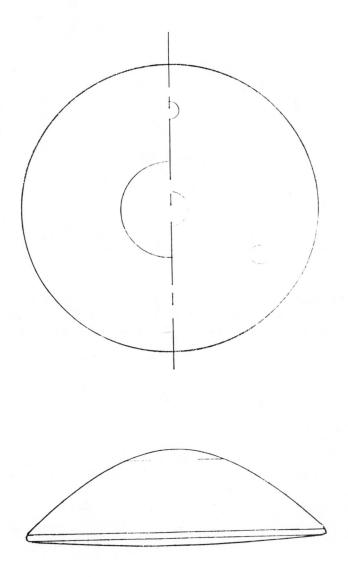

3 July 1967, 19:15, Cumberland, Rhode Island. Line drawing of a small craft that seems to have been launched from the open hatch in the underside of the cigar-shaped mother-ship.

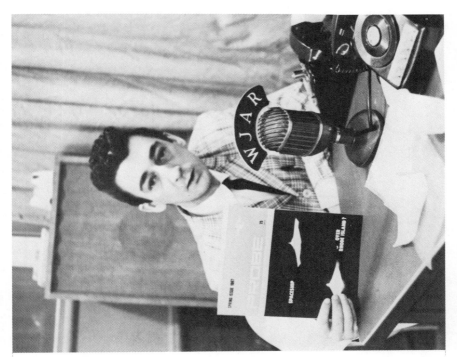

Joseph L. Ferriere, the radio announcer, and Ferriere holding the un-cut 620 negative strip of pictures.

61

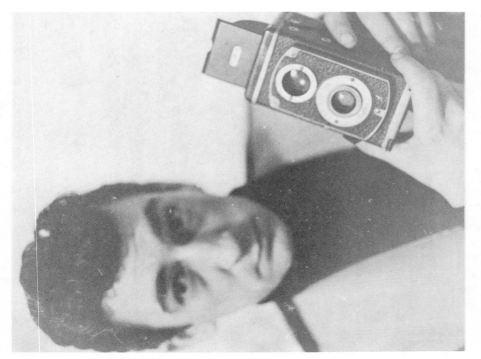

Joseph L. Ferriere with his camera, and the Pho-Tak 620 Reflex No. 1 camera used to snap these pictures.

3 July 1967, 19:15, Cumberland, Rhode Island. Photo No. 1 by Joseph L. Ferriere, printed in two densities and top slightly enlarged to show detail. Note the plunger in aft end to left, and belly hatch opened.

63

3 Jyly 1967, 19:15, Cumberland, Rhode Island. Photo No. 2 also printed
in two densities, one slightly enlarged. The craft moved in a rocking
motion, like a boat on swells. Note the plunger still extended out of
aft. Something was rapidly ejected out the belly hatch.

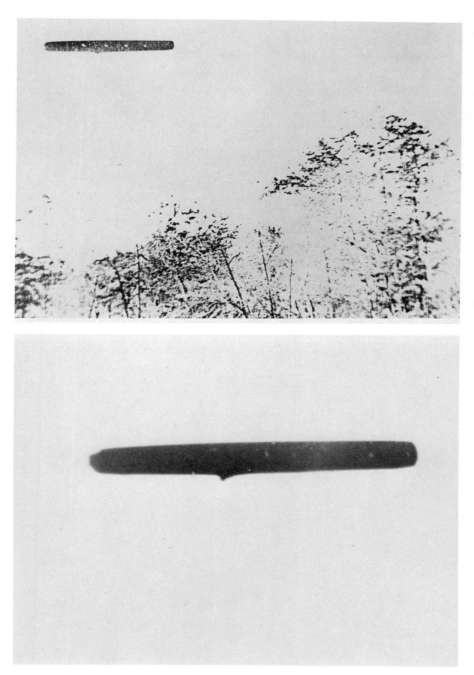

3 July 1967, 19:15, Cumberland, Rhode Island. Photo No. 2 in extremely high contrast to bring out spots along side and further enlarged to provide relative measurements on the ship. The object is drifting some closer and backwards, toward the left.

65

3 July 1967, 19:15, Cumberland, Rhode Island. Photo No. 4 again being shown in two contrasts. Note the lighter spots along the side in the highest contrast print. The visible roughness of the skin surface on the craft may be showing up in the highest contrast, top print.

3 July 1967, Cumberland, Rhode Island. Photo No. 4, softer contrasted prints, one enlarged, top photo. Note the aft plunger retracted. Belly port is still open.

3 July 1967, Cumberland, Rhode Island. Photo No. 5 in two different contrasts and sizes showing the small disc-shaped craft seen hovering to one side, after Ferriere had snapped the first photos of the larger craft.

3 July 1967, Cumberland, Rhode Island. Photo No. 6 showing the smaller disc-shaped craft beginning to leave. The white crescent is a flowmark on the negative. Photo No. 7, top, shows the cylindrical ship after it flipped to vertical and began rapid upward ascent in departure.

SAITAMA PREFECTURE, JAPAN
End January 1974

Near the end of January 1974, Hideo Takagi, eighteen
years old, from his home in the Katsushika District of
Saitama Prefecture, Japan, snapped 5 pictures of the
Japanese version of the Goodyear blimp flying overhead.
He was concentrating on the blimp and getting some good
photographs of it during the brief opportunity and that
was all he remembered seeing at the time. When he got
the developed prints back from the processor he was
surprised to see that in two of them he had captured a
dark cylinder-shaped object flying above the blimp. It
was very much higher and farther away but was clearly
registered in the film emulsion. Examination definitely
showed that this was not debris in the emulsion nor a
film flaw or developing defect. Another flying object
was clearly captured in the picture.

Single Photo

(This photo was irretrievably damamged in preparation for this volume)

End January 1974, Mid-day, Saitama Prefecture, Japan. Hideo Takagi,
eighteen years old, snapping pictures of a blimp caught this flying
cylinder high in the sky beyond.

YAIZU BEACH, JAPAN
6 May 1974, Morning

Mrs. Mitsuko Yasuzuka, a 40 year old teacher who lives
in Iwabune, was walking on Yaizu Beach on 6 May 1974,
when she decided to snap a picture of a large black rock
in the surf there. It was about 07:40 as she snapped the
two color pictures of the scene. Days later when the
developed prints came back from processing she was surprised to see that she had captured something else in
the beautiful scene. There was a huge cigar-shaped dark
object very high and far away in the sky beyond the big
black rock. The second picture made only a few seconds
later, showed the same darl cylinder much farther away
and nearing the horizon over the sea (too distant to
reproduce clearly here). Photo experts ruled out any
possibility of film flaw or developing defect here and
declared it a genuine object photographed far away.

6 May 1974, Morning, Yaizu Beach, Japan. Mrs. Mitsuko Yasuzuka photographing a black rock also captured a flying cylinder far beyond it.

71

KIRIGAMINE, NAGANO, JAPAN
29 July 1974, 10:00

At about 10:00 on 29 July 1974, a high school student
at Kirigamine, Nagano Prefecture, young Takayuki Hanawa
photographed a dark cylinder-shaped flying object above
a beautiful green field near the winter ski resort. He
was shooting the scene in summer garb. In this case a
dark spherical object, apparently launched from the big
cylinder was also captured in the same photo. Hanawa
did not notice either object at the time he was taking
the picture. Photographic experts examining the negatives declared that this was not a film flaw nor any
defect in processing, but that a real structured object
was photographed at a distance. There were a number of
other such photographs of dark cylindrical flying craft
made in Japan in early 1974.

29 July 1974, 10:00, Kirigamine, Nagano Prefecture, Japan. Takayuki
Hanawa inadvertently photographed a dark flying cylinder in the sky.
It was high above the beautiful summer scene he was photographing.

72

NAGOYA CITY, JAPAN
3 September 1975, 14:30

At about 14:30 in the afternoon of 3 September 1975, young Hirohito Tanaka, a 12 year old junior high school student was doing his homework in the living room of his house in Nagoya City. He happened to look up and out the big picture window and saw something flying high in the sky above the scattered clouds that day. Looking closer, he could see that it was a very unusual flying machine, dark and of cigar shape. He obtained a camera and quickly snapped 8 photographs of a huge dark gray cylindrical mother-ship that was launching and recovering smaller circular domed disc-shaped machines, some of which came down and flew low over the city.

The zeppelin-shaped mother ship was high and distinctly distant with the city haze graying the image noticeably. He continued snapping his pictures as some more smaller craft came out and some more went back inside of the huge cylinder. He was able to get both the carrier ship and some of the smaller circular ships in three of the frames exposed, but he also lowered his camera to capture more of the smaller ones in a group below the bigger craft, and then in different parts of the sky.

Now standing on the verandah there outside the picture window, Hirohito continued to watch the spectacle until the whole formation drifted away beyond his sight. He had seen both the cigar-shaped mother-ship and the small dark domed ships before, and he was to see them again.
(See the Nagoya City UFOs in this volume)

Kioshi Yazawa
KOZUMO Magazine, Japan

[Note that the shape of this cylindrical craft, slightly tapering toward the ends and then bluntly terminating is almost identical to the Palomar and Kilimanjaro photos.]

3 September 1975, 14:30, Nagoya City, Japan. Young Hirohito Tanaka snapped this photo from his own home.

THE NAGOYA CITY UFOs

Repeat sightings of UFOs by the same individuals has always been suspect, and repeat cases involving the same photographer of UFO craft are usually discounted and filed uninvestigated for the same fallacious reasoning.

One argument is that these are rare and happenstance occurrances, and that the chance of such accidental observations happening to the same party twice is too small to be significantly real and therefore too unreliable to waste time on. There is always a danger of being accused of gullibility if one takes such cases seriously and pays any attention to them. But there is such a case in Japan that is difficult to successfully dispute.

Mr. Hirohito Tanaka, 12, a student at Sakurayama Junior High School in Nagoya City has observed them almost a hundred times since he was 9 years old, and has taken dozens of photographs. Most of these times, he saw the flying objects and photographed them from his home and garden in Nagoya. He has also seen them from a river bank near his home. All of his family except his father (52) have seen the objects. His mother, Sachio (46) and brother, Toshiyuki (15) have seen them several times. He does not know why he sees them more than other people, but he is always trying to send telepathic messages to the sky as if he were conversing with them. He has seen many kinds of UFOs.

An entry in his diary for 26 March 1975, 06:00, says he saw a UFO in the eastern sky. This one was very big. Three round things were attached to the lower part of the ship. Another entry, undated, says he saw a large cigar-shaped mother-ship with three smaller ships flying around it.

And then, on 3 September 1975, he discovered a huge dark gray cigar-shaped mother-ship that launched and recovered smaller circular disc-shaped machines that came down and flew low over the city. It was 14:30 in the afternoon while he was studying in his house, that he looked up and out the big window and saw it flying high in the sky above the clouds that day. He obtained a camera and snapped 8 photographs of this object with some of the smaller ships in the same picture with the larger one.

Nine days later, on 12 September 1975, at 13:30, just after lunch, he saw 7 small circular craft with domes on top, as they maneuvered about in the southwest sky. He was inside his home this time also, when he saw them through the window, and he grabbed a camera and went out on the verandah and snapped several photographs before they flew away.

Almost a month after that, on 4 October, again in the early afternoon, at 14:00, he watched a bell-shaped ship come down close to the ground in a "falling-leaf" kind of descent, leaving a trail of white vapor or exhaust in its wake, then it leveled off and flew away horizontally out of sight. Again he ran to the balcony with his camera and managed to get several photographs of the craft. When the white trail drifted to the ground it was found to consist of spider-web-like filiamentary substance that evaporated away in a few minutes. The white material seemed to be ejected from the top part of the craft.

Two months after that, on 8 December, again at 14:00 in the early afternoon, he saw a small circular craft with a high dome flying in the sky to the southwest. He grabbed his camera, a Kodak Instamatic 126, and ran out into the garden and snapped a photograph of it. This ship had an understructure consisting of 3 hemi-spheres mounted on 120 degree spacing apart on the bottom surface of the vehicle.

Hirohito is not a particularly good photographer, and were it not for the simplicity of the Instamatic camera, he probably would not have gotten any pictures at all. He is not even interested in photography as a hobby. He takes his exposed film to the local camera shop in the neighborhood to have it developed. He uses mostly black and white film for its economy.

Other photographs were taken on 9 April 1976, at 14:00 in the afternoon, from the window of his room. He saw a small black circular craft with a high dome on top making a low pass over a neighbors house, and quickly shot 7 pictures in rapid succession. The object was moving in a zig-zag and falling-leaf fashion as it flew about in the sky. He could not see much detail, only noting its strange movements, certain that no conventional airplane could fly like that. This observation lasted 5 to 6 minutes altogether.

If there was a way to characterize trends in the multi-faceted UFO problem, one might say that a modern trend, since late 1973, would be repeated visits to the same locality and before the same witnesses.

Engineer D. Enrique Castillo Rincon, a well known business man and resident of Bogota, Colombia, has had more than a half dozen encounters with the same group of space entities since the evening of 3 November 1973. He was taken aboard their craft on more than one occasion. His story would fill a book alone. Across the Cordillera at Marcahuasi, Peru, Sr. Carlos Paz Garcia has been having a similar experience.

Back in Japan, the 11th of May 1975 marked the beginning of a series of UFO contacts with young Ryutaro Umehara, who lives in Chiba Prefecture. He had 3 experiences with 3 different types of craft on the same day, one at 09:00, one at 17:00, and another at 17:30 in the afternoon, and he took photographs each time.

Rincon reported experiences with 3 different types of spacecraft used by his visitors, and knows of even more in use by them here in our atmosphere. Tanaka has photographed at least 3 different types of craft in his contacts also, and so have many others. Where this is all leading it is difficult to specualte, but it is certain that we are in for more surprises in the future.

THE NAGOYA CITY UFOs

3 Sep 75, 14:30, Nagoya City, Aichi, Japan, Tanaka

12 Sep 75, 13:30, Nagoya City, Aichi, Japan, Tanaka

4 Oct 75. 14:00, Nagoya City, Aichi, Japan, Tanaka

8 Dec 75, 14:00, Nagoya City, Aichi, Japan, Tanaka

9 Apr 76, 14:00, Nagoya City, Aichi, Japan, Tanaka

NAGOYA CITY, AICHI, JAPAN
3 September 1975

At 14:30 in the afternoon, on 3 September 1975, young middle-school student, Hirohito Tanaka, 12 years old, was studying in the main room on the upper level of his house in Nagoya, when he glanced up, looking out the big front window, and was surprised to see, high in the sky above his home there in the city, a huge dark cylinder shaped flying object, bigger than a blimp and much above the altitudes flown by the blimps. It was dark gray in color and was moving along slowly above the clouds. He then noticed other small dark objects darting about in the sky near the cigar-shaped craft, and as he watched, he saw 3 more of the small dark objects come out of the larger ship, which then flew independently around the carrier-craft in company with the others that were already out there from before. Some went in and some more came out and flew around. One of the small objects then descended and made near passes over the city, and then he could see that it was circular and shiny, and had a small dome on the top of it. It did not land, but flew around at a lower altitude for a few moments and then went back up and rejoined the others. This spectacle continued until the whole gaggle of flying vehicles drifted away and out of sight altogether.

He went for his camera as he watched this strange aerial display over his city, and snapped 8 photographs before they were gone.

The developed prints clearly showed a large cylinder-shaped vessel high above the clouds and partially obscured in the haze and smog of the city between the ship and the camera. They also showed variously, different numbers of the small dark round objects flying around in different positions around the mother-ship.

This was not the first time he had seen this huge dark zeppelin-like ship in the sky. An entry in his diary for 26 March 1975 describes the sighting of a similar ship with three round things attached to the lower part. He has also seen these craft since taking the pictures, and is trying to make contact with them mentally.

From Jun-Ichi Yaoi

3 September 1975, 14:30, Nagoya City, Aichi Prefecture, Japan. Young student Hirohito Tanaka snapped photos of this cigar-shaped carrier crat launching and recovering small round objects over Nagoya City. A considerable distance away may be noted from the atmospheric graying.

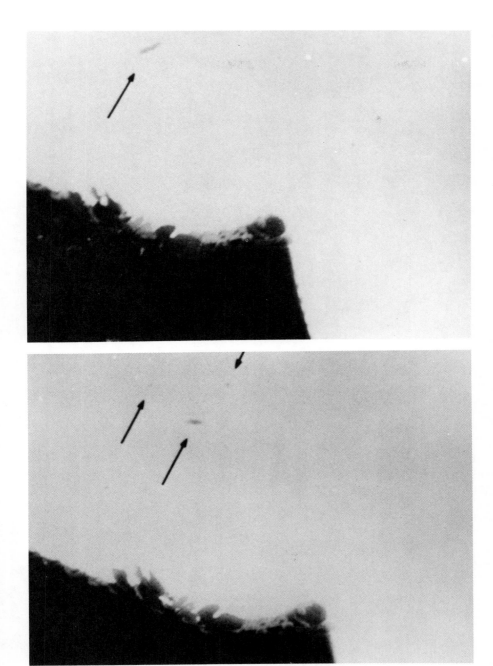

3 September 1975, 14:30, Nagoya City, Aichi Prefecture, Japan. High school student Hirohito Tanaka watched the smaller ships mill about above the city of Nagoya as he snapped more black and white photos of the moving objects. Some began to descend lower over the city.

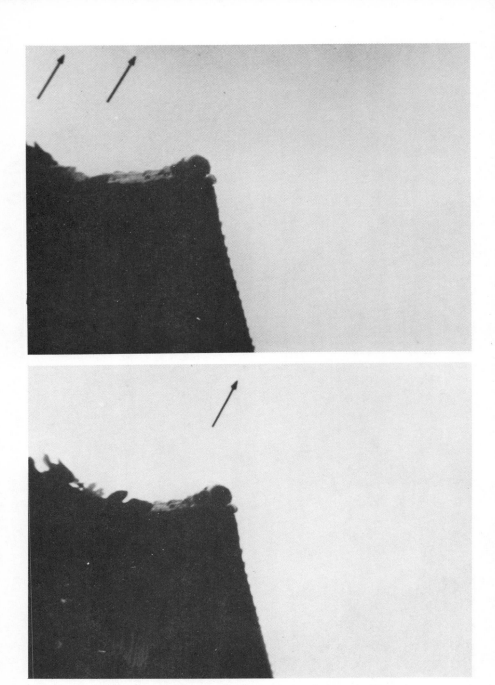

3 September 1975, 14:30, Nagoys City, Aichi Prefecture. As Hirohito Tanaka watched, some of the smaller objects came close enough for him to see that they were disc-shaped with raised domes on top. They also had some kind of visible protrusions on the bottoms of the craft.

3 September 1975, 14:30, Nagoya City, Aichi, Japan. The whole observation lasted about 7 to 8 minutes. The whole gaggle of craft drifted
away after the carrier ship, all moving away in the same direction.
The mother-ship drifted out of sight first.

NAGOYA CITY, AICHI, JAPAN
12 September 1975, 13:30

It was only nine days after successfully photographing
the carrier ship and its escort that Hirohito Tanaka saw
the small ships in the sky over his city again. It was
just after lunch when he happened to look outside and
saw the small disc-shaped flying objects again flitting
about and performing their by now familiar falling-leaf
maneuver. There were seven of them in the southwest sky
and they were disc-shaped with a raised dome on top. He
grabbed a camera and went out onto the verandah for a
better and less obstructed view. He was able to snap
several photographs of the objects before they flew out
of sight.

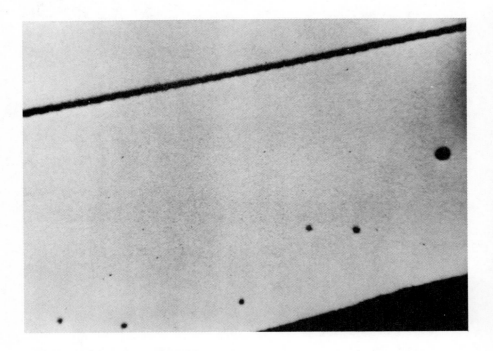

12 September 1975, 13:00, Nagoya City, Aichi Prefecture. Hirohito saw
these small dark craft flying around from inside his house and took
his camera outside to photograph them.

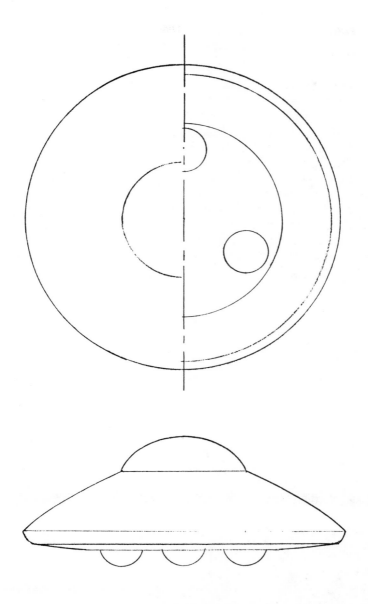

12 September 1975, 13:00, Nagoya City, Aichi Prefecture, Japan. Line drawing of one of the small domed disc-shaped craft that High School student Hirohito Tanaka watched descend over his house and fly about the local area. They flew erratically in all directions.

NAGOYA CITY, AICHI, JAPAN
4 October 1975, 14:00

At about 14:00 in the early afternoon of 4 October of 1975, high school student Hirohito Tanaka watched a small bell-shaped flying object descend to near ground level in a "falling-leaf" kind of motion. It left a trail of white vapor or exhaust in its wake as it flew. Near the ground it steadied, levelled off, and flew away horizontally until it was out of sight. Again he grabbed his camera and ran to the balcony where he managed to snap several black and white photographs of the ship. When the white trail drifted to the ground it was found to consist of spider-web-like filiamentary substance that evaporated away in a few minutes. The white material seemed to be ejected from the top part of the small ship.

4 October 1975, 14:00, Nagoya City, Aichi, Japan. Hirohito Tanaka, a local High School student, Saw the small domed disc-shaped craft once more, but this time the one was leaving a whitish trail behind it as it flew. The whitish material consisted of filiamentary substance.

NAGOYA CITY, AICHI, JAPAN
8 December 1975, 14:00

On 8 December 1975, again at 14:00 in the early afternoon, Hirohito Tanaka, a local high school student, saw a small circular craft with a raised dome on top as it flew around in the sky to the southwest of his home. He grabbed his camera, a Kodak Instamatic 126, and ran out into the garden where he managed to snap a picture of it. This ship had an understructure arrangement consisting of 3 hemi-spherical protrusions mounted 120 degrees apart on the bottom surface of the vehicle.

8 December 1975, 14:00, Nagoya City, Aichi, Japan. Hirohito Tanaka saw the small disc-shaped craft with the raised dome on top flying in the southwestern sky. This time he clearly saw an understructure on the bottom that looked like 3 hemi-spheres on tri-corner spacing.

87

NAGOYA CITY, AICHI, JAPAN
9 April 1976, 14:00

At about the same time as before, 14:00 in the early
afternoon, during his regular study time, on 9 April
1976, and again from the window in his home, Hirohito
Tanaka saw the small dark circular flying object with
the raised dome in the center. It was making a low pass
over the roof of his neighbor's house next door. Grab-
bing his Instamatic 126, he ran to the balcony and shot
seven pictures in rapid succession. The domed disc was
moving in zig-zag and falling-leaf fashion as it flew
about in the near sky. It was dark colored and he could
not see much detail, only noting its strange movements,
well aware that no airplane known to him could perform
such maneuvers. The observation lasted 5 to 6 minutes.

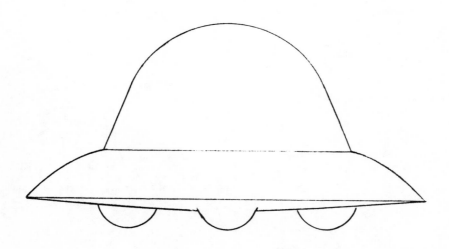

9 April 1876, 14:00, Nagoya City, Aichi Prefecture, Japan. This is an
enlargement from one of the seven black and white pictures snapped by
Hirohito Tanaka on this date. This ship made low passes over the roof
of his neighbor's house.

9 April 1976, 14:00, Nagoya City, Aichi, Japan. This is two of seven
black and white photos made by Hirohito Tanaka of a small lens-shaped
flying object as it zig-zagged over his neighbor's house. The object
came quite near the house on one pass.

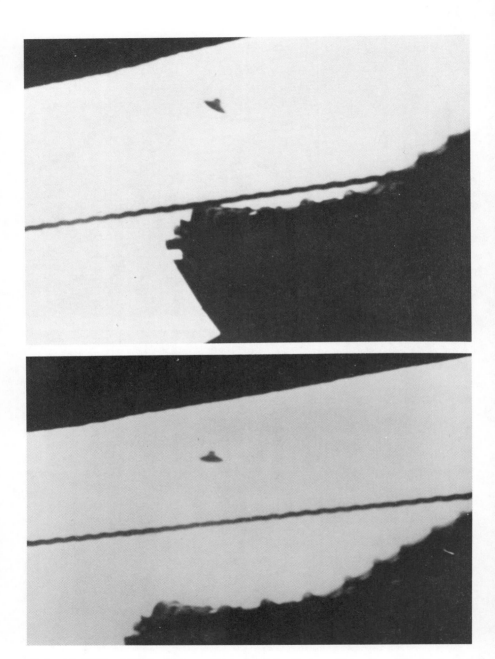

9 April 1976, 14:00, Nagoya City, Aichi, Japan. Two of seven pictures of the dark lens-ahaped craft with a dome on top seen flying at low level over a neighboring house as Hirohito Tanaka snapped photos. He used a Kodak 126 Instamatic camera.

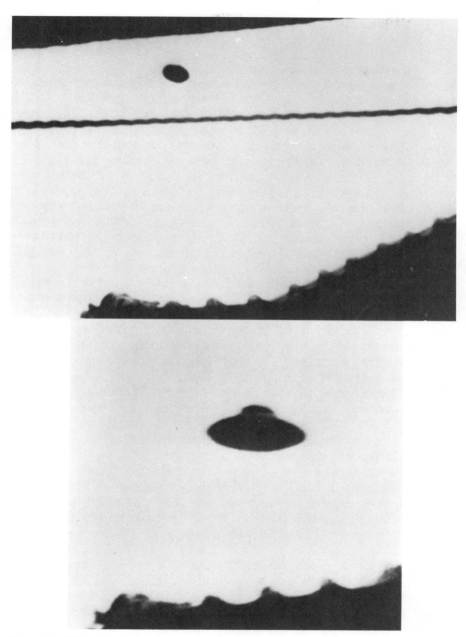

9 April 1976, 14:00, Nagoya City, Aichi, Japan. Two of seven pictures of the dark domed-disc that descended in a falling-leaf fashion and then zig-zagged around over a neighbor's house. Hirohito Tanaka was able to photograph it.

THE EAST WOONSOCKET, RHODE ISLAND, UFOs

The East Woonsocket - Cumberland, Rhode Island area has been a hotbed of UFO activity off and on many times in the recent history of UFOs. Ever since Harold Trudel's first accidental sighting of a UFO on
he has become obsessed with the need to find out and to prove the nature of the phenomenon. He was not particularly a believer before, but now he had to know and he went out looking every chance he could get. There were many sightings of strange flying objects and considerable activity was being reported from the local area in and around a scrub site on the edge of town. Trudel used his spare time both day and night searching this area for clues, and had another sighting while he had his camera along.
He managed to get photographs during the brief encounter and this only spurred him on. Other people saw and reported strange things in the local area and he collected these reports from all sources and tried to conduct what investigation he could. This brought him in contact with Joseph Ferriere, a local radio announcer who had recieved some calls about UFO sightings, and when he got his first photographes he went right to Ferriere with the evidence. Though hearing many reports, Ferriere was skeptical of UFO photographs right in his home town and doubled his efforts to find out about these. He arranged with photographers and technical experts to have these pictures analyzed for fraud. He was surprised to learn that they could find no evidence of fraud in the photographs. One expert went back out to the photo site and located every position from which the pictures were made and returned convinced that they would have been very difficult to hoax.
More reports came in and finally Ferriere bought himself a cheap camera and went out looking, and to his total and complete surprise got the Cumberland flying cylinder pictures of 3 July 1967. Trudel continued his investigations and saw strange flying objects again and snapped more pictures, one time in the company of Joe Ferriere who had gone out with him to an active location near the city. The activity continued and we have collected some of Harold Trudel's photographs here for you.

You have now read the story of Joe Ferriere's photos of the cylinder-shaped craft that launched a small silvery metallic domed disc that flew rapidly away and then returned and was photographed also. Ferriere was out in that particular area looking around because the radio station where he worked as a talk-show host had received a number of calls in the three preceeding days reporting a silvery bar, a metallic tube, a gray cylinder flying in the sky over the reservoir and scrub area. He simply went out to look around. He was already aware of other such reports from the area going on over a long period of time, and had good reason to accept some of these reports as valid. Ferriere himself was well known and respected in his community for his honesty and straight forward integrity.

One of those regularly reporting to Ferriere on these recurrent sightings was Harold Trudel. Trudel had heard reports of the UFO activity in the area more than a year earlier and had begun his own investigations until he saw his first one himself. From then on he became obsessed with finding answers to the enigma and haunted the area until he sighted one again. He began carrying his camera and finally got pictures of one of the objects. He reported this to Ferriere and brought him the photos.

Ferriere went out to the site with Trudel to look over the area and they both saw the small flying disc again and Trudel got two more pictures of that one in front of Joseph Ferriere. There was no longer any doubt in Joe's mind that something very unusual was going on. And that was the reason Ferriere bought the camera and went out again when the new flurry of activity started.

But by this time Harold Trudel already shot pictures of disc-shaped craft in that area three times. The craft Trudel photographed were slightly different in shape and style from the disc photographed by Ferriere, and Trudel never photographed any flying cylinders, though there were reports of them even then. Even the several craft, except in one instance, photographed by Trudel were of different style and size. This was in itself suspicious at the time because we had not yet learned that nearly all extraterrestrial operations over our planet involved a variety of special purpose vehicles of different shape and size.

Here then are some of Harold Trudel's UFO photographs.

WOONSOCKET, RHODE ISLAND
24 July 1966, 15:00

At about 14:45 on 24 July 1966, Harold A. Trudel, 28, of 147 Division St., Woonsocket, and a companion, Joseph L. Ferriere, also of Woonsocket, had gone out into the East Woonsocket area, near Diamond Hill Road, where Mr. Trudel had previously snapped black and white daylight pictures of a silvery metallic lens-shaped UFO with a raised dome on top. Trudel had seen strange flying objects of this kind in this area before that and there were a number of other reports of similar sightings by other people unknown to Trudel or Ferriere. They had been discussing the reports earlier that Sunday afternoon and decided to hike up into the area and see what they could find. They drove up the Elder Ballou Meeting House Road to the power lines. Leaving the car there, they hiked about two miles along the power lines right of way where Trudel had seen them before. Suddenly, at about 15:00, they spotted a lens-shaped object flying there in the sky, on edge, like a rolling coin.

"The first one came in from our left – we were facing, I would say, north-northeast," Ferriere said. "It was coming down at about a 45 degree angle. It was tipped so that its rim edge was perpendicular to the horizontal in travel. I was really amazed. It was very small; only appeared to be 3 to 4 feet in diameter, but we must have been almost 150 feet away from it."

He said it appeared to be about the size of a quarter held at arm's length, and was shaped like the lens from a magnifying glass.

"Harold sighted it through his camera and snapped a picture," Ferriere said. "While he was winding the film, the second UFO, the same size and shape as the first, arrived from our right. He raised his camera and snapped the second picture just as the two craft were meeting. As he was winding the film for a third shot the UFOs did a loop under the power lines, from right to left, and then sped off toward Cumberland – following the lines – at terrific speed."

Trudel took the roll of film to Dube's Pharmacy and they sent it to Jan's for processing and the negatives and prints were returned. The first shot showed only one small dark lens-shaped object above the power line wires in a near cloudless sky. The second shot showed two of the lens-shaped UFOs, one at wires level and the other below and passing under the wires. That picture was enlarged at Yvonne's Photo Supply to 8"x10" size. It did not show any more detail in the UFOs than in the smaller print, other than a greater indication of motion. It appeared that the two objects were beyond the nearest pole but much closer than the second pole. The negatives did not show any evidence of tampering. They both showed the same edge-fogging as the other pictures taken with this camera, which Trudel had purchased several weeks before this for $3.00 at a second hand store, thinking it to be a "good camera".

One print showed, besides the object, a 4 and 5 and the words "Verichrome Pan" and an overall mottled effect on the print. In the 2¼x2¼ inch negative the image of The UFO measures 1/8th inch from tip to tip. The numbers and lettering appeared on only the one frame.

Trudel allowed his camera to be examined. It is a simple snapshot affair, using 620 film, which was produced by a Chicago firm just after World War II. It has the appearance of a twin-lens reflex, but is actually a modification of the simple box camera. The shutter speed is slow, about 1/30th to 1/50th second, and the lens has a very small opening, although the glass diameter is about 3/4th of an inch. The camera is such that it would be virtually impossible to "fake" such pictures with it.

An interesting sidelight is the appearance of the numbers and the lettering on the developed film. When the events of that day were reconstructed, it turned out that the camera had lain face down on the seat of Trudel's car, in the sun, for several hours. The numbers and lettering matching that on the paper backing for the film, it was concluded that the red lens in the film transport window in the real of the camera had faded to a lighter shade and the sun shining directly through it caused the lettering on the paper to imprint on the film under the window at that time. This may also give us one indication of the expertise of this photographer at that time and his potential ability to create hoax pictures.

August Roberts

24 July 1966, 15:00, E. Woonsocket, Rhode Island. Harold Trudel this
time accompanied by Joseph L. Ferriere, a local radio talk-show moc-
erator, had gone back to the site of some earlier observations by Mr.
Trudel to look over the scene when two new type UFOs approached.

WOONSOCKET, RHODE ISLAND
9 November 1966, 23:00

At about 23:00 on the night of November 9th, Mr. Harold Trudel of Woonsocket, Rhode Island, was sitting in his car parked on Elder Ballou Meetinghouse Road in Woonsocket and was scanning the skies for the strange luminous object he had seen several times in both daylight and darkness, photographing it twice since snapping day photographs of another disc-shaped UFO in the same vicinity in the presence of UFO investigator and radio announcer, Joseph L. Ferriere, also of Woonsocket, on 24 July 1966.

Suddenly he spotted a "golden-yellow glow" coming up from beyond the horizon. A light or luminous object was moving very slowly, much like a satellite at first, although a "pulsating" effect was noted.

Having 4 shots left on his loaded film, he quickly snapped them, removed that film, reloaded, and readied the camera again. The object had moved somewhat closer now and seemed to be huge. Trudel noticed a "rocking" motion aa the UFO wavered from left to right. He started "snapping like crazy" to get as many pictures as possible and succeeded in getting 6 more pictures before the object disappeared.

As soon as he got home Trudel attempted to contact Mr. Leonard E. Brodt, also of Woonsocket, who has equipment for developing and printing and had offered his special services to Ferriere after developing out the other photographs made on 24 July in Ferriere's presence. Trudel had succeeded in getting night photographs twice since then which he had also taken to Brodt for developing, but the luminous object in both cases was too distant and the result was inconclusive. Unable to get in touch with Brodt, he took the roll of film containing the four first pictures to a local developing outfit the following day. Three days later, his film was returned fully developed EXCEPT for the last four frames! Upon inquiry he was told that the last four frames contained nothing! (This happens to UFO photographs far beyond any average for pictures in general)

Trudel, aware of the fact that other important UFO evidence had beel "lost" in the same manner, "sat" on the other roll of film until he could contact Lenny Brodt.

97

Brodt developed the second roll of film, and upon seeing the result immediately called Ferriere, who was also editing PROBE magazine. As soon as he could make prints he rushed them and the negatives over to Ferriere, by now followed by Harold Trudel who had joined him. They examined the photographic evidence and Trudel turned all the negatives over to Ferriere at PROBE where they were filed away under lock and key along with other UFO evidence held by PROBE magazine.

Those pictures and story were then published in PROBE magazine for Spring 1967, Volume FOUR, No. 1, Whole No. 18, pages 4,5 and 6. Ferriere and Brodt questioned Trudel for 3½ hours, recording the interview for PROBE. We may quote from the transcription of that dialogue that night:

Q. Since it was dark how did you manage to find the film numbers for the frame?

A. I used a flashlight. I always carry a flashlight in my car.

Q. These photos are time exposures; what was the length of each exposure?

A. I believe they are about three seconds, but the time might have varied one or two seconds on different exposures.

Q. Did the object advance, then recede at various intervals while you were filming it (the image in frame 4 is smaller than in frame 3).

A. That is hard to say. There was a pulsating effect, so that when the object brightened it appeared closer and when it dimmed it looked farther away, but I do not believe it was going back and forth, though it's possible. It appeared to be coming towards me.

Q. How many lights did you see on the object?

A. The whole thing was glowing with a golden-yellow light. At times I thought I saw dark "spots" in the middle, between the upper and lower portions. The thing was one big glowing mass.

Q. How long did you have it in sight?

A. That's a funny thing. It seemed like hours, but I guess it was really about 10-12 minutes. That's a very rough estimate because, somehow, I seemed to lose all sense of time.

Q. What were the weather conditions?
A. It was a clear, dry night, very dark. I do recall seeing some stars.

Q. Did the object appear to be solid?
A. At first it looked something like a flourescent light. When it came closer I could see it was definitely solid. I noticed a transparent effect periodically; but definitely a solid object.

Q. Did it appear blurred, fuzzy or sharply defined?
A. The object was very sharply defined. The object's edges were clear-cut, to me.

Q. Did the object appear to stand still at any time?
A. Yes, it did. But not for long. It had a rocking motion, even when it stood still, from what I saw.

Q. Did you see any smoke or vapor trail?
A. No?

Q. Did it change shape at any time?
A. No.

Q. Did it flash or flicker?
A. No. It was a slow pulsating effect.

Q. How did the object leave the area?
A. It started to move away, then gradually dimmed out to nothing. It went right back where it came from and I lost it over the horizon.

Q. Did you hear any sound?
A. I heard a very faint, I mean I could just about hear, what sounded like a vaccuum cleaner.

Q. Do you intend to file a report with the government, or any branch thereof?
A. No. I don't want anyone from the Air Force coming to my home and telling me I saw swamp gas or a temperature inversion. I've heard about the way they have ridiculed other observers and I don't want any part of that. I'm giving everything to you. If they want anything they'll have to contact PROBE. You know how to handle them.

As a result of the seeming authenticity of Trudel's photos, and because the area of activity was nearby, in

East Woonsocket, Leonard Brodt went to the exact location specified by Trudel on the evening of December 26th equipped with a 35mm AGFA camera to do some skywatching.

He sat in the car with the window open for about half an hour, when his attention was suddenly attracted to a bright, orange ball of light hanging motionless in the sky. He grabbed his camera, steadied it on the frame of the open window, and snapped two 4 second exposures of the UFO. He then grabbed his flashlight and camera and got out of the car on the driver's side. Standing in the road, he looked up and saw the strange object still in the same position. He raised his camera to take another shot but was amazed to find that he could not locate the object in the viewfinder. Looking directly he could see no trace of the mysterious lighted object. It had simply disappeared in an instant.

He noted that the Moon was behind him at the time of the observation, and estimates that the total duration of the sighting was about 45 seconds. This was Brodt's first observation of a UFO and it was very similar to the two photo events filmed by Trudel that failed to reveal conclusive evidence that what he photographed was if fact a UFO.

Brodt commented,"It was strange the way it just seemed to vanish. The UFOs are real and they are over East Woonsocket. Something strange is going on up there..."

This, of course, is well known by Trudel and Farriere as well because they had both heard of the UFOs over the East Woonsocket area before the 24 July event mentioned at the beginning of this report.

August Roberts
PROBE Magazine

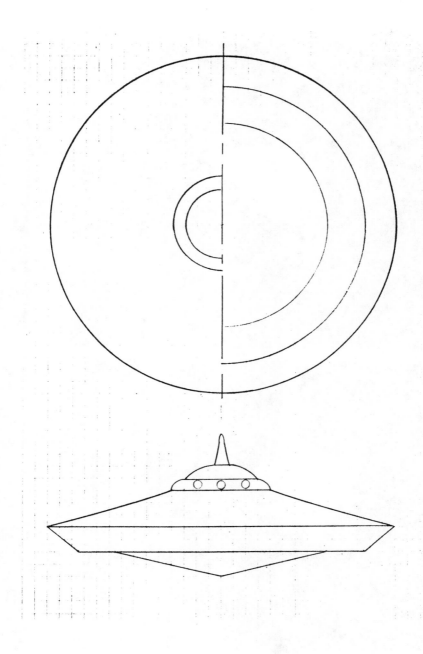

9 November 1966, 23:00, Woonsocket, Rhode Island. Line drawing of the UFO photographed at night by Harold Trudel. This was the third time he had observed and photographed this luminous body, but the closest time also, and was able to observe some detail in it.

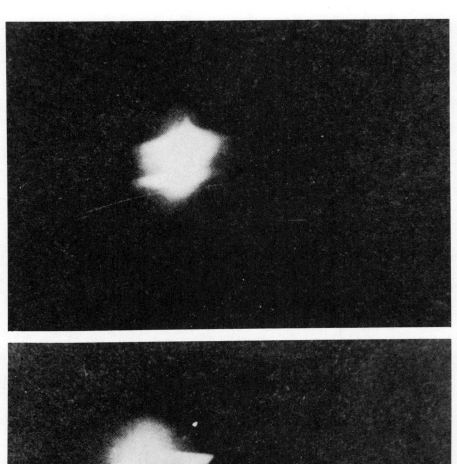

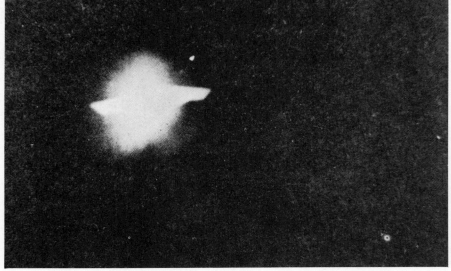

9 November 1966, 23:00, East Woonsocket, Rhode Island. Photos number 1 and 2 on the second roll of film used in the UFO photographic event captured by Harold Trudel. The last 4 frames on another roll of film of this same event were "lost" by the commercial processor.

102

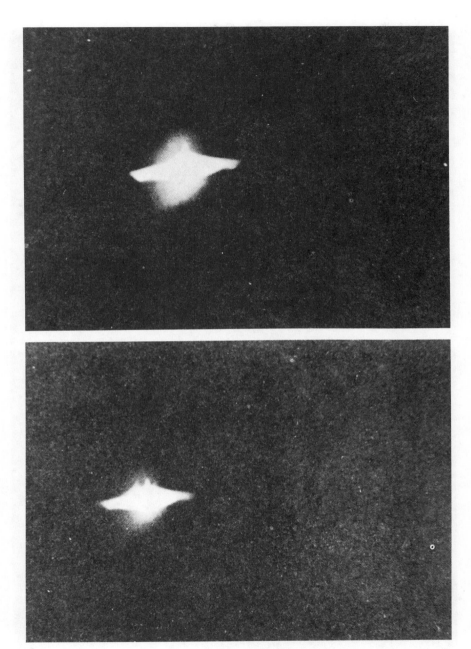

9 November 1966, East Woonsocket, Rhode Island, Photos number 3 and 4
of the saved roll of film shot by harold Trudel. Note that the image
of the UFO is smaller in No. 4 than in No. 3, due to either the pulsating intensity or possible fore and aft movement, undetermined.

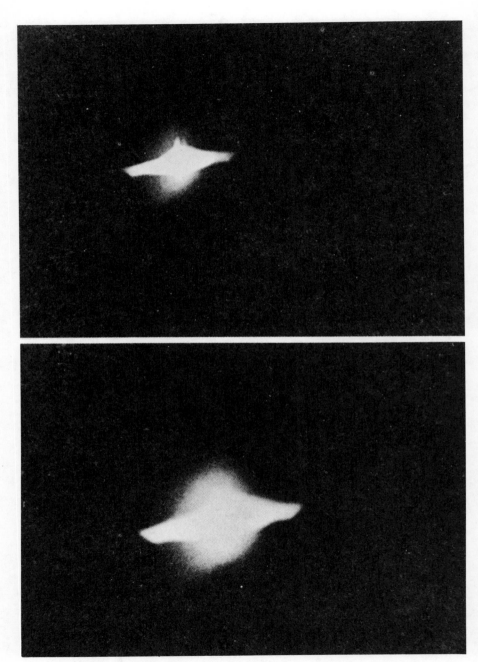

9 November 1966, 23:00, East Woonsocket, Rhode Island. Photos number 5 and 6 of the second roll of film shot by Harold Trudel that night. After this the object started to withdraw, dimmed and disappeared from view.

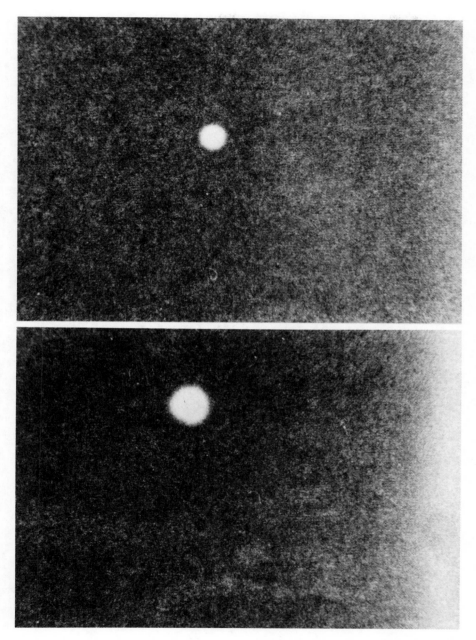

26 December 1966, East Woonsocket, Rhode Island. These are the two UFO photographs snapped by Leonard Brodt from the very same location as the 9 November pictures by Harold Trudel. Note that the object seems to have come closer or increased in brightness in the second photo.

105

WOONSOCKET, RHODE ISLAND
10 June 1967, 12:00

At about noon on 10 June 1967, Harold Trudel (29), a
local resident, when driving on west Wrentham Road, near
the high tension line, suddenly spotted a shiny silvery
metallic disc-shaped flying object with a high dome on
the top side. It was moving in a bobbing weaving motion
as he stopped the car and got out with his camera. He
quickly adjusted it and managed to shoot 7 good black
and white photographs of the object before it left the
scene. It approached quite close and almost hovered at
one time and he snapped three pictures in close sequence
at that time.

This multi-tiered disc form shaped more like a child's
humming top than a disc had a high raised dome on the
top which had a squared off top level with a small dome
raised on the top of that. The sides sloped in tiers to
the flat wider rim, and there was a smaller convex curved under surface with another larger central dome pro-
truding from the central bottom surface there.

The object rocked back and forth and changed up and
down elevations like it was on an ocean swell as it flew
around the witness. He had a good opportunity to see it
from all angles as he snapped the pictures.

These pictures were also taken to Joseph L. Ferriere
for analysis after being developed by Leonard Brodt who
again did all he could to verify the validity of these
pictures for himself.

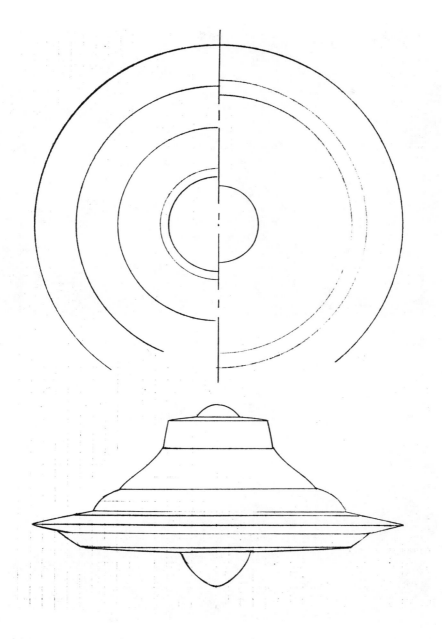

10 June 1967, 12:00, Woonsocket, Rhode Island. Line Drawing of the UFO photographed by Harold Trudel after he spotted it flying around the power lines along Wrentham Road. He was able to take seven pictures.

10 June 1967, 12:00, Woonsocket, Rhode Island. Harold Trudel saw this domed disc-shaped object flying over the power lines and stopped and got out with his camera. The object above the wires circled out and made a low approach from over the scrub out in that area.

10 June 1967, 12:00. Woonsocket, Rhode Island. Harold Trudel steadied his camera and snapped these two photographs of the object as it made its nearest approach to the witness in this photographic sequence. He took the pictures to Leonard Brodt for immediate development.

On 16 June 1967 Harold Trudel was back out in the bare scrub area searching for evidence of the object that he photographed only six days ago when he managed to snap 7 black and white photographs of a very similar or possibly the same ship. He was walking through the scrub when he turned to look and suddenly it was there, right behind him, close by, at low level near the sandy brush ground with its sparse tall grass and small shrub vegetation.

He raised his ready camera and got two good snapshots of the object as it moved slowly at first, then flipped up on edge and flew away.

Trudel has seen and photographed a variety of the disc shaped craft, both day and night, in and around Woonsocket. Others checking on his sightings have seen and even photographed similar things. There are many other reports from witnesses completely unknown to Trudel that were made from in and around that area at that time.

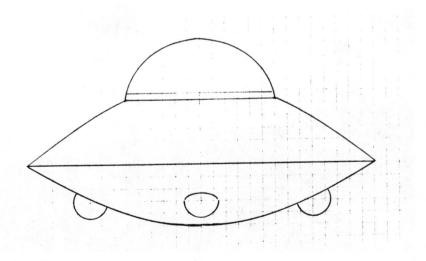

16 June 1967, Mid-day, Woonsocket Rhode Island. Harold Trudel managed
to get still another set of photographs of the hi-domed disc-shaped
metallic flying object very similar to or identical with the one seen
and photographed on 10 June 1067. Two black and white photos resulted.

WOONSOCKET, RHODE ISLAND
11 July 1967, Afternoon

On the afternoon of 11 July 1967, Harold Trudel was
back out in the East Woonsocket scrub area where he had
observed and photographed the strange disc-shaped flying
objects when he spotted another such craft flying higher
and farther away than had been his last experience. This
was still another new fourth type of craft, and this one
seemed to be of a larger diameter than the others, and
it had a lower profile also -- more disc-shaped than top
or bell shaped.

He managed to get one photograph of it during the very
fleeting sighting time available. The object was darker
on the bottom and lighter on the top. It was in a level
flight attitude and flew horizontally. All power failed.

11 July 1867, Afternoon, Woonsocket, Rhode Island. This is the only
surviving photograph of probably the 4th disc-shaped UFO type to be
photographed by Harold Trudel in this general area.

GEORGETOWN HARBOR, NEW BRUNSWICK, CANADA
June 1968, Early Morning

On an undetermined day in June of 1968, Leo McCabe was walking in a relatively deserted scrub area with his small plastic Brownie camera, a model that uses 127 size film, when he spotted a shiny metallic-looking circular object flying at low level. It was slowly turning around a vertical axis as it moved along over a foreground of scrub branches and sparse tall grass under an overcast sky. It had a prominent raised dome on the upper surface and a flatter dome on the underside. This object flew fast at times, estimated to be above 300 mph in quick spurts, and it also hovered nearly still, as when he was able to snap his two pictures. This object is very similar to the 10 and 16 June 1967 photographs by Harold Trudel of Woonsocket, Rhode Island. McCabe snapped his pictures near Georgetown Harbor, New Brunswick (PWI).

McCabes pictures were printed in TRUE F.S. #3, 1969.

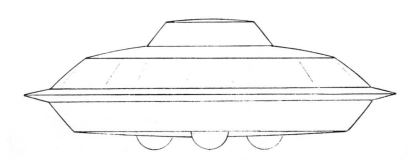

June 1968, Georgetown Harbor, New Brunswick, Canada. Profile drawing of the domed disc photographed as if flew over a sparse scrub area. The object is very similar to one photographed at Woonsocket, R.I. in June 1967 by Harold Trudel.

June 1968, Georgetown Harbor, New Brunswick, Canada. Two photographs of the silvery disc-shaped flying object observed and snapped by Leo McCabe as it flew over a deserted scrub area. Note the similarity to two sets of UFO photographs by Harold Trudel of Woonsocket, R.I.

NEEDLE-SHAPED UFOs

There is another class of cylindrical UFOs that are better characterized as needle-shaped because of their extreme thinness to length ratio. They are quite large, being hundreds of feet long and never coming close to the surface of the planet.

This type of craft was reported as far back as in the Mahabarats and Ramayana, epic documents of ancient India where they were called Vimanas, and "flew with the power of the sun". They were described as slender needle-like forms of brightly reflective metal that travelled from planet to planet.

But they apparently still come to this planet because at least 11 witnesses in 3 different locations observed such an object in the skies over Phoenix, Arizona at noon on Thursday the 12th of May 1977, and two of those witnesses snapped color photographs of the spectacle. None of those people could offer any suitable explanation as to what it was, having independently ruled out the things that it looked most like to each of them.

Ms. Evelyn McGurk, a resident of the Spanish Gardens Apartments on North 32nd Street, was the first to notice the object in the sky. She was sitting on the north side of the swimming pool sunning and half dozing as she faced toward the east. She had seen an airplane go over a half hour earlier and had watched the contrail it left dissipate. It took only 2 or 3 minutes for it to disappear completely. Now she opened her eyes again and saw what at first looked like another contrail, only this one was very short, later reconstructed to be about an inch long measured between the thumb and forefinger held at arm's length. It also looked more solid and had very smoothe, sharp outlines, and it was darker on the underside and very bright on the upper surface. And this one didn't seem to be dissipating. She opened her eyes several more times in the next 5 minutes, curious about its unusual persistence, and then she noticed that it was moving around to a different place each time she looked. She called Mr. Jacques de Bove's attention to the object and asked him what he thought it was.

Jacques, another resident of the Spanish Gardens, also sunbathing by the pool, looked and saw it moving and

115

puzzled over it, and then decided it was really something unusual. Thinking of a friend who was interested in UFOs, he hurried to apartment 66 to tell Mr. Lee Elders before it got away. Meanwhile, Evelyn had called Mrs. Ilse Schrott's attention to the object. Ilse and her husband "Digger" were also sunbathing by the pool. "Digger: went to their apartment and brought out a pair of Opera Glasses for better viewing, but they were not strong enough and little advantage was noted. The 3 continued to watch the object as it moved back and forth and then went up higher. It also moved sidewaysfrom left to right and back. Ilse said it looked silver and was shaped like a cigar. She said she saw it move sideways and also back and forth. She said it seemed very steady in the sky and looked and moved much like the zeppelins she had seen in Germany when she was a young girl, except that this one also moved sideways. It was lower when she first saw it and it moved up higher.

Then Jacques returned with Lee Elders, Tom Welch and Vance Irwin, all from Elders' apartment. Lee and Tom watched for only a moment and then ran for their cameras and were followed by Vance Irwin. Tom's camera was ready and loaded with film so he grabbed it and returned to the pool area where the others were still watching the object, having been joined by more spectators who were now also watching. Lee's camera was in a box on a shelf in the clothes closet and had the lens off, and it was not loaded with film. He had to install the lens and load the film before going back outside. Meahwhile, Vance Irwin was standing on the patio outside Lee's bedroom window keeping an eye on the object which was at this time descending lower and he thought it would go ᴜown behind the rear fence wall before Lee got out there with his camera. He kept urging Lee to hurry.

When Lee did get out there the object was low down to the right of a large palm tree, in a position just above a lower palm leaf on the right side of the tree. He shot the first picture there. Then it began to ascend and to move to the left a little. He snappec the second photo only a few seconds later and the object had already risen above the highest fronds of the palm tree. It continued to rise, and just a few more seconds after the second picture he snapped the third as the object was now seen high above the highest fronds of the palm. He

116

and Vance watched for about 10 to 15 seconds more as it continued to move to the left to above another palm tree about 10 degrees azimuth from the last. Here Lee snapped the 4th photograph. He was watching the object through the telephoto viewfinder and was about to snap a fifth picture when the object just disappeared. He did not see it fade out or shrink, now did it withdraw, and he did not see it go anyplace. It just disappeared as he was watching it.

Meanwhile Jacques de Beve had returned to the pool where he continued to watch the strange object with the others. He said that after Evelyn had called his attention to it he saw it make 2 short jumping movements to the right. Evelyn was talking to Ilse and they missed this movement. He decided then that this was no ordinary contrail, and when Ilse went to her apartment to get some better binoculars he ran to Lee's apartment to get Lee and his camera to take a picture of it. Returning to the pool area with them he had stayed to continue his sunbathing and to watch. Jacques said that when he first saw the object it was between the tops of the two groups of palm trees to the east by southeast. It moved slowly to the north (left), descending a little as it moved. Then it reversed its travel and moved back to the south, making two quick jumps to the south as it otherwise moved at the same slow pace. Then It began to rise straight up, making no change in pitch angle or inclination, and that is when he ran for Lee Elders.

By the time they had returned to the pool it was quite high up in the east, about 70 degrees elevation, and then it began to descend again and to the right, coming down slowly. He also saw it change size 2 or 3 times, but the change was quite rapid and it returned to its original size almost immediately. The change was in a lengthwise direction and just momentarily. It continued to descend slowly to the right until it was down to almost 20 degrees elevation, and then began to rise verticaqlly again, and then its ascent began to curve to the north as it rose. Mr. Elders began taking pictures with his camera about the time it began this last ascent before vanishing. Elders snapped the first 3 pictures only 3 or 4 seconds apart, and the last one about 10 seconds later. (Elders actually snapped 5 shots but the first one was the first on the new roll of film and two

117

thirds of it was lost in processing. The part remaining did not contain the object. For the purpose of this report we mention only the 4 whole frames obtained.) When the object vanished as Lee was watching it through the viewfinder for another shot, Jacques was observing the object rising in the curve to the north and was looking directly at it when it suddenly "spurted" to the northwest and out of their field of view. That was the last they saw of it.

Vance Irwin, meanwhile, had gone back inside Lee's apartment to telephone his son John to tell him to go out and look for the object in the southwest. The Irwin home is 1.8 miles due north of the Spanish Gardens apartments. John was unable to spot the object at first and went back inside. Two or three minutes after that first call, Vance called John back to see if he had seen it. Upon getting a negative reply, he tried to describe the position again, and John went outside once more. As he got out into 32nd Street to look southeast, he saw a straight white elongated oval to his west at about 50 degrees elevation and moving northwest a little faster than the speed of an airplane. He saw a darker spot in the center of the oval. John saw the object bobbling along slowly from side to side as it moved toward the northwest. He said it was shiny on top and darker underneath. He could see slightly different angles as it wobbled in flight and he definitely felt that it was circular. Since these details did not fit the object being photogrphed, we may conclude that there was also another object associated with the one that was photographed by Lee and Tom.

Tom had gone back out to the pool as soon as he picked up his loaded camera, and began shooting pictures at a leisurely pace. He first saw the primary object at about a 40 degree elevation to the east-southeast. It at first looked to him like an aircraft contrail except that it was very short and didn't seem to be dissipating as he expected. It measured only an inch between his thumb and finger at arm's length. It also seemed brighter than any contrail he had ever seen before. It also had a very definite shape that was uniform and symmetrical. The ends of the object thinned down to a point exactly the same on both ends, and the curve to the point was concave, or curved in or together from the ends to a point.

118

Tom shot the first two pictures with a standard 55 mm lens, and then changed to a 75 to 250 mm zoom lens for the rest of his pictures. He had seen the object himself for over 4 minutes and if it was a contrail it had not changed shape at all. At times it seemed to glisten like a spider web glistens in the sunlight. He shot the first two pictures from the west steps down to the pool, then changed lenses and shot another from the side of the pool. He saw it glisten again and thought of a spider web between two of the palm tree tops, or a thin shiny wire, so he walked east to a point beyond the trees and the object was still there as big and bright as ever, but now it was moving to the south and descending, probably the same descent that Vance was observing as he tried to hurry Lee. It continued to descend until it was out of sight behind the trees to the group at the pool. Tom Estimated that it went down to as low as 10 degrees elevation at this point. And then it started to rise again, and when they could see it once more it was rising almost straight up but beginning to curve up to the north.

At this point Tom saw it flicker or glint again and it momentarily got longer, almost twice as long, but it flashed back to the same size almost immediately.. Tom then walked farther east to get it into a clear sky area for better viewing as he continued to shoot pictures leisurely. Now there were no trees for suspension of wires or webs. He felt that the object was about a mile away to the east at this time. He had to re-focus his camera because the image had gone out of focus due to object movement, and then he shot another picture. He was framing the image in his viewfinder for still another shot when it just disappeared as he was looking at it, and he did not see it again. Jacques who was also watching it at that moment, said that it zipped off to the west as a streak from a standing start, and was gone for good.

The next day when Evelyn McGurk went to work at the Grenada Royal Apartments, one block away to the north, she was surprised to learn that Mike Placentia, a yard boy there, had seen the same thing at the same time and had gone inside to tell Betty and another employee, and they all went out to see it. They saw several of the sunbathers around the Grenada pool also watching the unununusual object.

119

Lee's Camera was an Olympus OM-1 with a Zuiko Auto Zoom 1:4 75 to 160mm lens with a 2X adapter. Tom's was an Asahi Pentax Spotmatic II. For the first two shots he used a Takumar 55mm 1:1.8 lens and for the rest he used a Vivitar Zoom 75 to 260mm 1:4.5 lens. Neither used any filters and both shot at 1/125th second with matching needle apartures.

When the developed photographs were recieved they confirmed the statements in every detail. Upon examination with a magnifying glass, something unseen with the naked eye was discovered. Three or more white spheres of the same brightness and of a diameter half the observed thickness of the object were moving rapidly in the space around the larger object. That they were moving very fast could be detected by observing the distance traveled by one of them in the 1/125th second shutter speed. Two of them maintained proximity in two of the photographs.

About this time a University Hospital lab technician living in north Tucson began to see almost identical needle-shaped objects in the skies northwest of Tucson as he drove home from work just after 18:00 daily. He didn't see them every day, but did observe them 3 or 4 times in the next two weeks. He became so concerned about them that he began carrying his camera to work to get some pictures next time they appeared.

On the 29th of May at the usual time, 18:00, on his way home, Bruce Zimmer once more spotted the strange needle-shaped flying objects to the northwest as he drove north up 1st Avenue. He had his Minolta pocket autopak 50, Instamatic 110, camera with him, and it was loaded with Fuji color negative film. He swung west over to Miracle Mile and continued north past Ina Road, then west again to Camino La Oesta, where he again turned north and drove to the end of La Oesta. From there he could look out across the desert toward the northwest with a clear view of the objects. He had driven over 6 miles north from where he had first seen them and they still seemed to be more than that distance beyond.

There were two of these needle-shaped objects looking like solidified clouds in appearance but as regular and geometrically uniform as big needles in the sky to the northwest, which he had been watching as he drove. When he stopped and got out of his car he saw another one

120

coming from the east. Then looking back at the first two he saw the lead craft dip down at a 45 degree angle and descend a ways then level off again. The second one began to overtake it. Looking back again, he saw two more coming from the east and crossing north of him toward the west. Then he noticed a strange effect. One and then another would lengthen momentarily and then shorten up again. They always returned to the same length. He could not tell whether this was from changing angle with respect to him or whether the change was actual. One then another would overtake and then fall back again. The objects were completely silent and were white on top and gray underneath, looking exactly like very well defined, very coherent short segments of airliner contrails, except they were in the wrong place for such. They reflected the sunlight brilliantly, and occasionally glinted. Sometimes they stopped dead still in the sky for long minutes at a time.

Bruce watched them for over two hours until they faded out at sundown and could not be seen. They became dark against the fading blue sky as the shadow from the sunset passed them, and were then absorbed in the dark. Bruce was able to take six photographs with his small format camera before it got too dark for his lens. When the prints were developed it was possible to pick the strange objects out in the sunset sky, but because of the nature of the lens, its poor low light sensitivity, the lateness of the hour, the small film size and the long distance away, the pictures are nothing spectacular to study. In fact they do not even reproduce well enough to print them here. It is possible, however, to discern that the objects photographed by Bruce Zimmer are almost identical to the one photographed over Phoenix with much better equipment.

Bruce Zimmer knows nothing of Lee Elders or Tom Welch, and they know nothing of him

But a clincher came only a few weeks later When Ray Stanford was riding an airliner from El Paso to Phoenix, which passes close to Tucson on its route. At some point about east of Tucson, Ray was idly looking out from his window seat, toward the east, when he spotted a strange needle-shaped object that looked like cloud substance but it was geometrically very regular, like a solid object, and was flying along at the cruising altitude of the jetliner. He had his 8mm movie camera in his lap at the time and, recognizing something very unique and very different about this cloud, he picked the camera up and began filming. He exposed a few seconds of film with the regular lens in position. Then he stopped and rotated the turret mount to bring a telephoto lens into position for a closer view. He noticed that it glinted or flashed occasionally and tried to catch one of the flashes on film, and actually succeeded in doing so.

When he got the developed film back and projected it for examination, he discovered that when he had rotated the lens turret to the telephoto position he had also brought a polarizing filter into play, which happened to be mounted on the telephoto lens at the time, and he had polarized images on the second part of the film. When he got to the flash he discovered also that the flash was an explosive discharge of accumulating energy from one end of the object and then the next discharge from the other. He could distinguish the energy accumulating on one half of the object to a full charge point and then the discharge with a glint and a sudden extension of the length in that directionn and then a contraction to normal again. He also discovered that there was in fact a solid meedle-shaped object inside the ionized field which gave a sort of a cloud-like appearance but always like a tight sheath around the object. The discharge was always straight out from the end of the object and was visible for a distance about equal to the length of the object. Also he could see that at the point of discharge a shadowy ring, distinguishable only in the polarized segment, formed around the ahip ar right angles to the direction of discharge. This ring was about the length of the solid inner object in diameter, and only persisted for a moment after each discharge.

Now these are truely strange flying objects indeed and just may be the vimanas of the sanscrit epics once again visiting our small insignificant planet. In this case, some questions raised about the details of the first sighting of this type are cleared up to some extent in the succeeding reports.

This class of unidentified flying objects was not only seen here, however. They were reported and photographed

122

over Japan as early as 1961, and they weren't accepted very well by the UFO groups around the world at that time either.

On 21 December 1961, Mr. Y. J. Matsumura riding on JAL (Japan Air Lines) Flight 307 (DC-4) from Fukuoka to Tokyo, while over Mount Aso, at 16:30 in the afternoon, saw and photographed two huge thin needle-shaped whitish objects in the sky maintaining pace outside his airliner window. As he watched, a smaller round dark object emerged from the forward craft of the two and made an approaching pass on the airliner off the right wingtip and then disappeared behind the airplane. The larger craft manitained position for a few more seconds and then dropped back and disappeared

Almost the same kind of event was repeated a little over one year later, and it involved the same Yusuke J. Matsumura, a UFO contactee living in Yokohama. At 12:45 on 12 February 1963, Matsumura, a passenger on a Boeing 727 All Nippon Airways airliner flying at 7,000 meters over Japan, photographed two white cigar-shaped objects paralleling the airliner's flight path. One of these very slender, almost needle-shaped, objects released a small round dark object that flew towards the airliner and then flew away. Matsumura snapped photographs with a Minolta SR-7 camera having a 58mm f1.4 lens at 1/250th second shutter speed.

Three and a half years later, on 22 June 1966, another picture was made of one of these needle-shaped UFO craft. It was about 11:00 AM when Mr. K. Furudate snapped four photographs of a huge slender cloud-covered object moving independently of other clouds in the sky. He was riding as a passenger on ANA Flight 240 cruising 15,000 feet above the Seto-Inland Sea, near Osaka, Japan, and snapped the pictures through the airliner window. he was using a Nikon 35mm camera with a Nikkorex zoom lens. The photographs were made at 1/250th second at f.8 with Y-52 and L-38 filters.

We wonder how many similar photographs are out there in private albums and small collections that have never come to the attention of the public.

NEEDLE-SHAPED UFOs

12 May 1977, 12:00, Phoenix, Arizona, Elders - Welch

21 Dec 1961, 16:30, Fukuoka-Tokyo, Japan, Matsumura

12 Feb 1963, 12:45, Air Route, Japan, Y. J. Matsumura

22 Jun 1966, 11:00, Osaka, Japan, K. Furudate

12 May 1977. 12:00, Phoenix, Arizona. Two photos by Tom Welch with his Asahi Pentax Spotmatic II camera. Top- First photo with standard 55mm lens mounted. Bottom- After lens change to 75-250mm zoom lens. Object is about 40 degrees elevation toward the southeast.

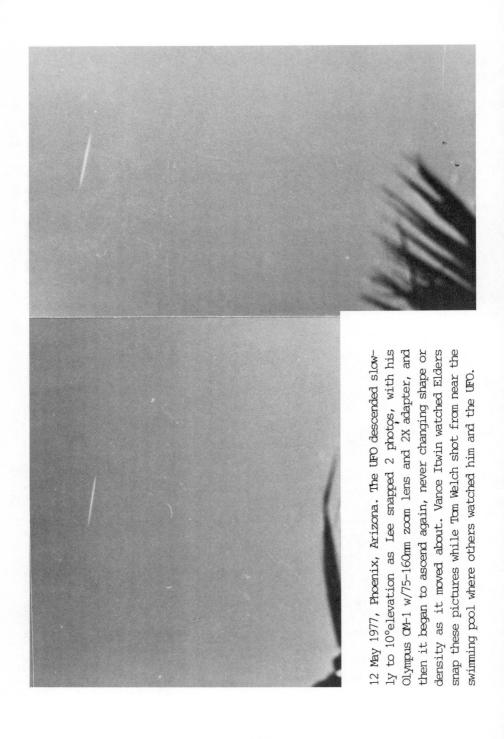

12 May 1977, Phoenix, Arizona. The UFO descended slowly to 10°elevation as Lee snapped 2 photos, with his
Olympus OM-1 w/75-160mm zoom lens and 2X adapter, and
then it began to ascend again, never changing shape or
density as it moved about. Vance Itwin watched Elders
snap these pictures while Tom Welch shot from near the
swimming pool where others watched him and the UFO.

12 May 1977, 12:00, Phoenix, Arizona. Two more photos by Lee Elders show re-ascent of the strange object.

FUKUOKA-TOKYO, JAPAN
21 December 1961, 16:30

At about 16:30 in the afternoon of 21 December 1961, as Mr. Yusuke J. Matsumura, riding as a passenger on JAL Flight #307, was passing near Mount Aso, he happened to look out the window of the plane and was surprised to see a slender almost needle-shaped "cloud" of a distinct color paralleling the airliner's flight path and maintaining pace with it alongside. He watched through the sirliner's windows, and when he thought that the strange cloud was moving differently from the other clouds out there, he raised his camera and snapped a photograph of it. The needle-shaped cloud maintained its position on the airliner for a few more seconds and then dropped back and disappeared.

21 December 1961, 16:30, Fukuoka-Tokyo, Japan. Looking out the window of JAL Flight #307 on which he was riding, Yusuke J. Matsumura saw a strange "cloud" of different color and moving independently of the other clouds in sight, and snapped a picture of the phenomenon.

AIR ROUTE, JAPAN
12 February 1963, 12:45

At about 12:45 on 12 February 1963, the same Yusuke J. Matsumura, who lives in Yokohama, was riding as a passenger on an All Nippon Airways Boeing 727 jetliner flying at 7,000 meters, as he again gazed out the airliner window, suddenly spotting two needle-shaped slender whitish cloud-like objects paralleling the airliner's flight path. He raised his camera and began snapping pictures of this unusual phenomenon. Suddenly one of the cloud-like objects released a small round dark object that flew towards the airliner and then flew away. Matsumura was able to get a picture of the cloud-like object with the dark flying sphere in the same frame.

12 February 1963, 12:45, Air Route, Japan. A little over a year later, Y.J. Matsumura again riding an airliner witnessed almost the very same spectacle. He saw the needle-shaped clouds release a dark sphere which approached the airliner and then flew away.

OSAKA, JAPAN
22 June 1966, 11:00

Another picture was made of one of these cloud-like or mist-shrouded needle-shaped flying objects on 22 June 1966 when Mr. K. Furudate observed the phenomenon and snapped four photographs of these slender objects moving independently of other clouds in the sky. It was 11:00 in the morning and he was riding as a passenger on ANA Flight #240, cruising at 15,000 feet above the Seto-Inland Sea near Osaka. He snapped the pictures through the airliner window using a Nikon 35mm camera with a zoom lens. The Pictures were snapped at 1/250th second at an f.8 aparture setting.

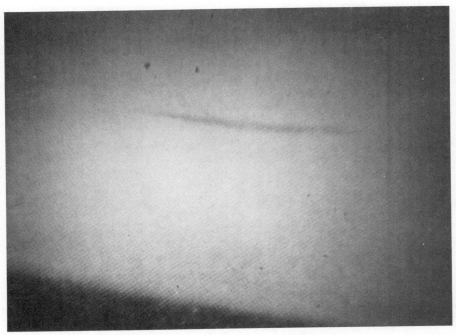

22 June 1966, 11:00, Osaka, Japan. Mr. K Furudate riding an airliner 15,000 feet above the Seto-Inland Sea near Osaka observed the same needle-shaped clouds and snapped four pictures through the airliner window. These closely resemble the clouds that launched the sphere.

Cigar-shaped UFOs will be distinguished from cylinder-shaped UFOs by their rounded or pointed ends and a somewhat fatter midsection. They are more blimp-shaped and have a greater diameter for length whereas the cylinder-shaped UFOs are characterized as more slender for their length and having truncated or squared-off ends, like a cigarette.

A typical example of a flying-cigar is the ship photographed over Puerto Maldonado, Peru on 19 July 1952, at 16:30 in the afternoon by Peruvian Customs Inspector, Domingo Troncoso. He observed and photographed a huge cigar-shaped craft flying horizontally, low in the sky, and it was leaving a dense trail of what looked like a rolling cloud of smoke. That object was real, a huge craft, several hundred feet high in the sky, as seen by its relfection cast in the slowly moving waters of the Madre de Dios river in the foreground of the picture beneath the object. A similar cigar-shaped craft flying at about the same low altitude over a Marysville, Ohio, school yard full of playing children, emitted a dense cloud of substance much like the one in this case, and that occurred in about the same years. This substance upon reaching the ground was found to consist of a mass of flax-like fibres that dissolved to the touch.

On 17 September 1954, at 17:45, a huge cigar-shaped object was photographed over Rome, Italy. First came a noise like the roll of approaching thunder, up close, which grew louder as the object neared. Thousands of Roman citizens heard it and located the source, a short cigar... or rather half-cigar, shaped object high in the air above the city.

Then the noise stopped and the object stopped, or appeared to stop, and just hung there in the sky at an altitude of around 6,000 feet. It remained there stationary for a while, certainly for minutes, and then suddenly shot upward, trailing an exhaust of milky-white vapor. It rose vertically and disappeared going straight up, leaving only a streamer of smoke as evidence of one of the most authenticated cigar-shaped UFO cases ever recorded.

The observatory at Ciampino described it as a flying

cigar oriented vertically on end, with the smaller end to the bottom. Something like an antenna was observed on the top as it hovered in this attitude. The Italian Defense Department said it was a sort of a shortened cone with the narrower end down.

It wasn't only the speed with which it disappeared that astounded observers; but the fact that it was able to hang vertically, still, in the sky for some several minutes, and apparently without any expenditure of Power of any visible kind. It was recorded on Radar sets in the area for 39 munites. It was silver colored on one side and red on the other. It treveled northwest. At one time it came as low as 1,000 feet altitude above ground. Associated Press correspondent Maurizio Andreolo and an International News Service correspondent Michael Chinigo as well as United States Ambassador Clare Luce Booth all witnessed it. Chinigo said. "I saw with the naked eye the mysterious glying 'cigar' which flew over Rome and which clearly registered on Radar sets in the area. To me it seemed like an inverted, sawed-off cone... what was strange was the object's ability to 'park' in mid-air for several minutes."

On the 11th of November the United Press reported more than 400 UFOs had been reported throughout Italy in the previous 60 days. This followed immediately on the heels of the great UFO wave of France in 1954 where cigar-shaped craft were also reported.

At Darmstadt, Germany, on 28 February 1957, at 13:30, in broad daylight, Mrs. Sigrid Brandt snapped a picture of a huge cigar-shaped UFO in flight.

On an unidentified night in December of 1957, Ralph Nicholson saw and photographed a luminous cigar-shape in the sky over Patterson, New Jersey. The observation and photography were made through a 3" telescope.

A spectacular photograph of a cigar-shaped UFO was made in Argentina on 7 February 1963. Sr. Felix Carrizo and his wife were driving their automobile South on hi-way Route 5 from Buenos Aires to La Pampa. At a time around 18:30, in the evening, as they came over a rise near Alberti, they saw a stupendous sight. They could see a huge cigar-shaped craft hovering in a near vertical attitude above a pasture with some cows in it. It looked to be silvery metallic in color and had lights along the side. It was of immense size, which Carrizo estimated to be over 600 feet long. It had a bright glow at the lower end. It was inclined to near vertical position, just like a satellite launching rocket. Carrizo pulled over and stopped his car and he and his wife sat there and watched the spectacle for a minute or two. They were staggered by the sight. Here was an object as big as a Moon-launch vehicle, hovering in launching position over a pasture with no launch equipment oa any kind and no support facility, and it was launching itself unaided! It began to rise slowly, leaving an exhaust like an Apollo launch vehicle. When he could recover Carrizo got his camera and snapped one photograph of this unforgettable sight as the ship was rising. It accelerated rapidly and flew up and out of sight. The whole observation lasted three and a half minutes.

CIGAR-SHAPED UFOs

19 Jul 1952, 16:30, Puerto Maldonado, Peru, Troncoso

7 Feb 1963, 18:30, Alberti Heights, Argentina, Carrizo

PUERTO MALDONADO, PERU
19 July 1952, 16:30

At about 16:30 in the afternoon of 19 July 1952, the attention of Customs Inspector, Sr. Domingo Troncoso, then with the Peruvian Customs Office at Puerto Maldonado on the jungle frontier with Bolivia, was called to a very strange cigar-shaped flying object over the river area. The big dirigible-shaped craft was flying horizontally and fairly low in the sky, passing from right to left from the observers position. It was leaving a dense trail of thick smoke, vapor, or substance of some kind on its wake. The thick whitish substance appeared to be emitted from the aft end of the object in flight. That this object was a real, structured, physical machine may be seen from its reflection in the waters of the Madre de Dios river underneath it. It can be clearly seen to be well above the broad-leaved jungle trees along the bank of the river in the foreground of the picture. The object was estimated to be over a hundred feet long.

Sr. Troncoso obtained a camera and was able to get one good photograph of the cigar-shaped object.

19 July 1952, 16:30, Puerto Maldonado, Peru. The Troncoso photograph.

135

Late in the afternoon of 7 February 1962, at about
18:30 local time, Sr. Felix Carrizo and his wife were
driving their NSU Prinz automobile westward on Route #5
from Buenos Aires toward La Pampa. They had been driving
steadily at normal speed for some time and pulled off
the road for a short rest stop.

It was then that Sra. Carrizo noticed to the right of
them, a strange aerial vehicle drifting their way. It
was a stupendous craft, still some considerable distance
away over the trees, and was floating at a steeply inclined attitude angle with the horizon. It was inclined
at about 80 degrees above the horizon, sloping only ten
degrees from zenith, and was drifting in the air a few
score meters above the pasture and trees in that location. Carrizo estimated the slender cigar-shaped object
to be about 200 meters long and 20 meters in diameter,
a fabulous size for this singular object.

As it got closer he could see that it had a silvery
gray metallic color, and was cylindrical in shape, with
a row of six rectangular "windows" along the side which
were brightly lighted from inside. The second and third
"windows" from the front (upper end) glowed brighter
than the others. The light from these panels was so intense that it hurt the eyes to look directly at the
brightest parts of them.

Remembering his camera, an Alpha-Alnea, in the trunk
in the rear of the vehicle, Felix ran for it, got it out
and readied it and took one photograph of the spectacular machine. When he lowered the camera he could
see that the huge object was beginning to rise. It had
developed a bigger glow at the lower end and ascended at
ever increasing velocity (with successive impulses), at
its steep 80 degree angle of inclination, until it was
quite high, then it changed its angle to slightly less
elevation and disappeared from view still climbing into
the evening sky. The pastoral scene with grassy meadow
and trees and cattle grazing returned to its peaceful
quiet as though nothing had happened.

An object bigger than the Saturn-boosted Moon-mission
vehicles of Earth had launched itself from the surface

136

or our planet, over a quiet countryside, with NO sophisticated launch platforms, gantry equipment or facility
of any kind, and didn't even leave any visible trace of
its visit.

Carrizo's black and white photograph clearly shows a
huge luminous cylinder just above the near horizon of
trees in silhouette against a darkening sky, with ground
level dust and haze illuminated to a dim glow by the
extreme brilliance of the light from the craft.

A point about 30% from the nose of the ship, in about
the position of the second rectangular "window", is so
brilliant that it flares out detail in that area on the
craft. It also produced light flares in the lens system
of the camera in their correct positions with respect to
the high intensity source of light and lens characteris-
tics of the camera used. A reflected glow from the object is also seen in the meadow grass on the near side
of the silhouetted trees.

One would have expected the photo effort to fail completely considering the lateness of the day, low incip-
ient light, extreme brightness of the light from the
object and ordinary quality of the camera used, yet
the photo is quite clear.   There was just enough daylight left and enough light from the object to result in
a spectacular shot. An 8" x 10" print from the original
negative was furnished for this report by Sr. Guillermo
Carlos Roncoroni of the E.I.F.E. UFO study group in the
city of buenos Aires.

The camera used was an economical Alpa-Alnea 7, with
a Schneider Alpa-Xenar 1:3.5/75 telephoto lens, 1/250th
second exposure, f:16, on Kodak Plus-X Panchromatic Type
B 35mm film.

From Sr. Guillermo Carlos Roncoroni, E.I.F.E.

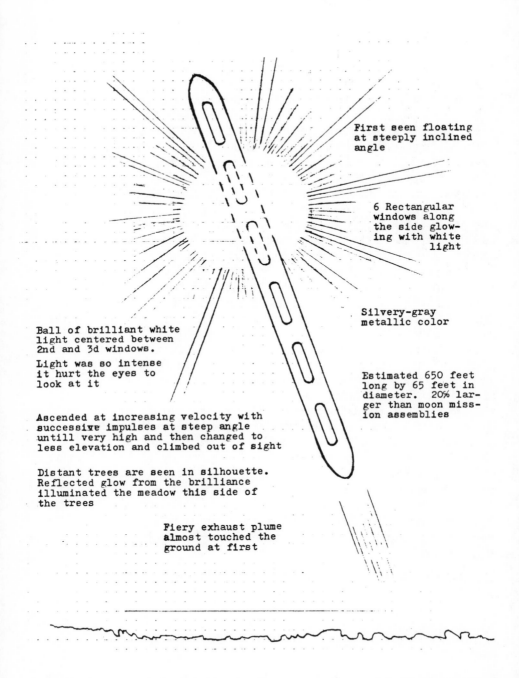

First seen floating
at steeply inclined
angle

6 Rectangular
windows along
the side glow-
ing with white
light

Silvery-gray
metallic color

Ball of brilliant white
light centered between
2nd and 3d windows.

Light was so intense
it hurt the eyes to
look at it

Estimated 650 feet
long by 65 feet in
diameter. 20% lar-
ger than moon miss-
ion assemblies

Ascended at increasing velocity with
successive impulses at steep angle
untill very high and then changed to
less elevation and climbed out of sight

Distant trees are seen in silhouette.
Reflected glow from the brilliance
illuminated the meadow this side of
the trees

Fiery exhaust plume
almost touched the
ground at first

7 February 1963, 18:30 Alberti Heights, Buenos Aires, Argentina. This
sketch, approved by the witness, shows what he described as having
seen visually as he was preparing to snap the photograph.

7 February 1963, 18:30 Alberti Heights, Buenos Aires, Argentina. The one photograph made by Carrizo.

CAPSULE-SHAPED UFOs

In the transition from spherical to cylindrical or cigar-shaped UFOs we have an intermediate shape which may
be described as an extended sphere or a cylinder with
rounded ends, a shape very similar to the medicinal capsules sold in drugstores. And we have this shape reported for UFOs also.

The first of this type to be photographed was over the
Japanese community of Fujisawa City, a suburb of Yoko-
kama on the morning of 20 August 1957. Mr. Shinichi
Takeda and his sister Kyoko were standing in the small
garden ajacent to their house at about 11:20 in the
morning and then Kyoko saw a strange cylindrical object
with blunt rounded ends flying high in the sky above,
and indicated it to her brother. It was silvery bright
in color and looked like a metallic cucoon or capsule.
It seemed to give off a glow and reflected the sun like
metal. The craft was moving slowly high in the sky above
the city and beach area, flying at an estimated 3,000 to
4,000 meters (12,000 to 15,000 feet) above them and was
moving in a southerly direction.

Shinichi ran for his camera and prepared it for the
shot. When the object was directly overhead, it made a
90 degree turn and increased its speed from about 250
kilometers per hour to about 500 kmh. Mr Takeda was able
to snap 3 pictures on black and white film before the
object disappeared behind the clouds. The entire observation lasted about two minutes in all. The developed
prints showed the object near the top of a big cumulous
cloud buildup approaching thunderhead size

About that same time, 15 bathers at Enoshima Miami
Beach nearby spotted the same or a similar object passing over them at high speed. No sound was heard with either sighting.

The next one photographed, ten years later, on 27 June
1967, was almost identical in configuration and proportion, and was also a bright silver color that reflected
the sun's rays. Mr. Jefferson Villar of Union City, New
Jersey, snapped 6 color pictures of a clearly defined
solid looking capsule-shaped object in the sky as it
passed at low altitude over his house and wires in the

yard. He estimated it to be flying at between 1,500 and 2,000 feet altitude above the ground.

Then we have a change in the appearance of this type. The silvery reflective capsule shapes seemed to be replaced by a luminous or radiant variety. Now no blunt cylindrical shapes were reported photographed again untill December 1970. The new objects were about the same shape and proportion but now they were luminous orange in color and were almost always photographed under an overcast of clouds. Perhaps they would have appeared bright and shiny metallic in full sunlight. The action seemed to have shifted to the Southern Hemisphere.

At Cinco Saltas (Five Falls), Argentina, at about 6:30 in the evening of 26 December 1970, Sr. Octavio Cruz observed and photographed a brilliantly luminous capsule-shaped object flying lazily along at a 20 to 30 degree elevation above the horizon in the late afternoon sky. He snapped two color photographs of it as it moved from right to left, changing the pitch angle of the nose of the craft as it flew along

The new type of capsule-shaped object was next observed and photographed back in Japan where the first pictures were made. On an undetermined day in August 1973, at Kure, Hiroshima Prefecture, F.S., a fifteen year-old schoolboy of Kure City (who declined identification), while taking a picture of the night sky, observed and photographed a brilliant luminous capsule-shaped object entirely by chance. He had his camera set and ready for a star picture when the object flashed into view leaving a faintly luminous trail behind it in the sky. The object shows up clearly against the dark heavens, The photographer was using a Nikomat FTN camera with a Nikkor 50mm f1.2 lens.

Any doubt about the relationship between the silvery metallic capsule-shapes and the glowing orange ones was to some extent alleviated by this next case. A silvery, reflective, capsule-shaped flying object that was not self-luminous at first, was photographed less than a month after the Kure picture, and in a daylight sky. Mr. Hitoshi Mizutani, 17, staff member of a company, took one color picture of a mysterious shiny metallic capsule

141

Flying over Sayama, Saitama Prefecture on 2 September 1973. It was about 17:30 in the afternoon, and as he watched, the object changed color to a reddish then to orange in about 5 seconds. He shot the picture with an Asahi Pentax SP camera with a Takumar 50mm f1.4 lens set at f4 and 1/500th second exposure on Fuji N100 color negative film.

Then back around the world to Argentina there was a report of another glowing orange object of this shape.On 30 May 1975, an Army Colonel from the Cuartel General (General Headquarters) in Buenos Aires (equivalent to our General Staff at the Pentagon) saw a similar capsule shaped object over the city and snapped 3 good color photographs of it. This craft was self-luminous and ra- diated a bright orange color. The fact that he succeeded in getting any pictures at all is remarkable because the sky was dark and drizzly all day on the 30th of May, and was not good for the kind of camera and the type of film available at the time. This officer insists on complete anonymity for the reason that he is on the Army General Staff and his government does not take an official posi- tion on the UFO question. (His true identification is on file with the authors) This case came to light is a very strange way.

On 17 June 1975, an employee of ONIFE Central, a local UFO investigative organization located at Gaona 1312, Capital Federal, upon opening the office for the day, discovered an envelope on the floor. It was sealed and had apparently been slipped under the door sometime dur- ing the night. Opening the letter, he found three 35mm color transparencies and a note describing a UFO sight- ing experience. The letter is translated here by per- mission of ONIFE:

"The object of this letter is to deliver (3) diaposi- tives made on Friday the 30th of May of this year.First, I must remain anonymous. I belong to the official head- quarters of the Argentine Army. You understand the prob- lems publicity would give me."

"On 30 May, I had lunch at home with my wife and two children. The day was dismal and the sky was completely overcast. About 14:00, thinking that it was unusually dark for that hour of the day, I went up to my room to dress, and on an impulse, lifted the curtain a little to

142

look out, **and there was the light** that shows in the photos. I looked for several seconds, then decided to continue dressing as I was running late. While dressing, I returned to the window to look again and the light was gone. In a few seconds however, I saw it rising from behind the water tank on the neighboring building, and then it descended some again and stopped. Then my son entered and seeing me at the window, came and looked out also. We watched and discussed it for a couple of minutes. My son thought it might be a UFO and suggested we take a picture of it. I obtained and prepared the camera and took the first picture, mostly to satisfy him. After taking the picture the light began to descend again, slowly, until it disappeared behind the water tank once more. I set the camera down and continued dressing while my son watched out the window. In a few seconds he said that the light was coming back. It was in the same place and had the same color and luminosity, which was quite bright, and it was moving as I took the second picture. It was moving toward the east and beginning to ascend when I snapped the third picture. My son called to my wife and my other son who came up and saw it also. My son insisted that it was a UFO, an opinion which I did not share at the moment. While we were discussing this, the light accelerated and disappeared toward the east at such velocity that I could not react fast enough to take another photograph."

"That is how it happened. Several days later, on the 8th of June, I went, with my family, to the Olympic Theater to see your audio-visual exhibit. That convinced me that we must have seen a UFO. I made copies of the photographs and am sending you the originals for study. Untill this time I did not believe in the existence of 'Flying Saucers'. Now I do."

The ONIFE investigation conducted by Sr. Guillermo Carlos Roncoroni made the following points:

1. The three transparencies were all made with the same camera settings.

2. All three photographs were underexposed due to the darkness of the day.

3. An emulsion study showed that the transparencies were developed in too high a temperature or too long in the first developer.

4. There were no aberrations in the emulsion.

5. There was no double exposure or montage.
6. Rechecking the weather, ONIFE found that it rained all day the 30th of May over Buenos Aires.

This was an experienced military officer of high rank, well educated and trained in their war college, an expert observer by anybody's standards. We would be hard put to find a more qualified witness. But he was not the only witness to such objects.

Two months later, on 23 July 1975, at 05:05, early in the morning, near Crepy-en-Laonnais, Aisne Province of France, M. Jean Bonnet observed and photographed an almost identical capsule-shaped object of the same shape, proportion and luminous orange color. No other details are available.

Almost one year after that, at 18:30 in the evening on 9 May 1976, the luminous orange capsules were again photographed over Argentina. Ms. Silvia Marie Weber was walking along Pehuenco Beach in the Province of Buenos Aires, about 60 kilometers northeast of Bahia Blanca, when she noticed several people observing a strange luminous yellow-orange capsule-shaped object flying slowly in the late afternoon sky above the beach area. She went for her camera and returned in time to snap one color picture of it before it flew away. A similar, or the same, object was seen at Tres Arroyos, 70 kilometers northeast of them only minutes later.

Then another set of pictures of the unusual capsule-shaped glowing orange UFO was reported in Argentina but this time there was a new twist to the phenomenon. This time the photographs showed a large yellow-orange ship with two yellow-white luminous objects of smaller size flying around the larger one as the whole gaggle moved along under an overcast sky. These three color slides were made by a Commodoro of the Argentine Air Force who, because of his position (as was the case with the Army General Staff Officer), insists on complete anonymity. (His true name and address are on file with the author.) This officer took these pictures about 20 kilometers to the south of Alberti in the Provence of Buenos Aires on 28 May 1977.

The Comodoro was driving his automobile when his teenage son first spotted a brilliantly luminous orange colored capsule-shaped object flying slowly from north to south under the overcast clouds that late afternoon. The time was about 17:45 local according to his wristwatch. The father, trying to see the object also, stopped the car and got out with his camera, a Practika Pentacon 50mm hand held model. Before he was able to take the first picture, two brightly luminous yellow-white objects came out of the capsule-shaped "mother-ship" and started flying around it. Then another came out and they began to fly behind the larger object. The Comodoro began quickly snapping pictures, but almost immediately after launching the smaller craft, the larger ship disappeared into the clouds above followed by the smaller objects.

Now this sighting alone is remarkable because it is not often that more than one object is captured in a UFO photograph, but in this case, the "mother-ship" was observed in the process of launching smaller craft which then flew around independently and were actually photographed in the sky with the "mother-ship", the only such photos for a capsule-shaped UFO. The objects were estimated to be at least 2 kilometers away from the witness.

We have had reports of cylinder-shaped, cigar-shaped, and needle-shaped UFOs launching smaller objects but this is the only known case of capsule-shaped craft also launching smaller ships.

CAPSULE-SHAPED UFOs

20 Aug 1957, 11:28, Fujisawa City, Japan, Takeda

27 Jun 1967,　　　 Wichita, Kansas,　 Jefferson Villar

26 Dec 1970, 18:30, Cinco Saltas, Argentina, Cruz

　 Aug 1973,　　　 Kure City, Japan, Anon

 2 Sep 1973, 17:30, Sayama, Japan, Hitoshi Mizutani

30 May 1975, 14:00, Buenos Aires, Argentina, General

23 Jul 1975, 05:05, Crepy-en-Laonnais, Fr., J. Bonnet

 9 May 1976, 18:30, Pehuenco Beach, Argentina, Weber

28 May 1977, 17:45, Alberti, Argentina, Comodoro

FUJISAWA CITY, JAPAN
20 August 1957, 11:28

At 11:28 in the morning of 20 August 1957, Kyoko Takeda
was working in the small garded by her house in Fujisawa
City, a suburb of Yokohama, when, looking up, she saw an
unusual cylinder-shaped object with rounded ends, like a
medicine capsule, flying high in the sky above. She just
stared in surprise for a few moments and then called to
her brother Shinichi and pointed it out to him. It was a
bright silvery in color and looked like a big metallic
cucoon. Besides reflecting the sunlight brilliantly, it
seemed to give off some light of its own. The craft was
high in the sky above the city and beach area, flying an
estimated 3,000 to 4,000 meters above them in a southern
direction.

Shinichi ran into the house for his camera and back,
prepared it for the shot, and when the object was directly overhead he carefully centered it in his viewfinder and snapped the first picture.

Then the object made a 90 degree turn and increased
its speed from about 250 kilometers per hour to about
500. Shinichi was able to snap 3 pictures on black and
white film before the object disappeared behind the big
cumulous cloud near it. The entire observation lasted
about two minutes.

At about the same time, some 15 bathers at Enoshima
Miami Beach nearby, noticed a similar, or the same, capsule-shaped object flying above them at a high speed. No
sound was heard during either sighting.

In Shinichi's second picture the object has turned to
a different angle with the sun, and is seen as a darker
body in the shadow of some higher cloud matter.

20 August 1957, 11:28, Fujisawa City, Yokohama, Japan. Shinichi Takeda and sister Kyoko photographed UFO.

WICHITA, KANSAS
27 June 1967, Day

On 27 June 1967, during a period of high UFO activity in and around the local area and vicinity, Mr. Jefferson Villar, of Union City, succeeded in photographing the bright silver colored capsule-shaped object that passed over his head. It was brilliantly reflecting the sun's rays like metal and was making a strange noise as it flew along. Villar managed to get his camera into action and snapped 6 good color photographs of the clearly defined cylindrical structure with rounded ends. It looked to be solid and real as it passed at low altitude above a house and telephone wires. Villar estimated the object to be flying at between 1,500 and 2,000 feet above the surface at that point. We have been able to obtain only one of the pictures so far, and we have not seen any of the others.

27 June 1967, Day, Wichita, Kansas. Jefferson Villar observed and was able to photograph this capsule-shaped flying object passing above the roofs and utility wires in his vicinity.

CINCO SALTAS, ARGENTINA
26 December 1970, 18:30

At about 18:30 in the evening on the 26th of December 1970, at Cinco Saltas (Five Falls), Argentina, Octavio Cruz observed and photographed a brightly luminous capsule-shaped object flying slowly along at an elevation of 20 to 30 degrees above the horizon in that late afternoon sky. He was able to get two color pictures of it as it moved from right to left, changing the pitch angle of the nose of the craft as it flew along.

The object was so light in a light sky that it is very difficult to reproduce here, being all but invisible in any but the original print. In the second photo the capsule-shaped light shaded object is visible about one quarter inch above the second tall tree-top spike from the left.

Guillermo Carlos Roncoroni

26 December 1970, 18:30, Cinco Saltas, Argentina. Sr. Octavio Cruz was able to snap two color photographs of the luminous capsule-shaped UFO which he observed flying near Cinco Saltas.

KURE CITY, JAPAN
August 1973

On an undetermined day in August 1973, At Kure City, Hiroshima Prefecture, Master F.S. a fifteen year-old schoolboy of Kure City, who declines identification, was taking a picture of the night sky, when entirely by chance he observed and photographed a brilliantly luminous capsule-shaped flying object. He had his camera set and ready for a star picture when the unexpected object flashed into view in the night sky. It was quite bright and was leaving a luminous trail behind in its wake.

In the developed print the object shows up clearly against the dark heavens. The photographer was using a Nikomat FTN camera with a Nikkor 50mm f1.2 lens mounted.

Kiyoshi Yazawa

August 1973, Kure City, Hiroshima Prefecture, Japan. F.S. a fifteen-year-old Japanese schoolboy snapped this color photo of a luminous capsule-shaped UFO that flew into his night photography of some stars.

SAYAMA, JAPAN
2 September 1973, 17:30

A shiny silver cylindrical object with rounded ends was observed flying over Sayama, Saitama Prefecture of Japan on the afternoon of 2 September 1973. It was about 17:30 in the afternoon when the capsule-shaped metallic craft was first observed. It was simply a structured vehicle reflecting the sunlight in a daylight sky at first, and Mr. Hitoshi Mizutani, 17, a staff member of a company prepared his camera to take a picture of what he was observing. As he watched, it began to change color to a reddish and then to orange in about 5 seconds. His camera now ready, he took one color photograph of the mysterious craft. He shot the picture with an Asahi Pentax SP camera with a Takumar 50mm f1.4 lens set at f4 and 1/500th second exposure on Fuji N100 film.

The developed print showed the object in a stage of changing color from red to orange and now appearing to

2 September 1973, 17:30, Sayama, Saitama Prefecture, Japan. Hitoshi Mizutani, 17, was able to get one photo of this bright capsule-shaped flying object as it changed from silver to orange in color in flight.

On 30 may 1975, a senior Army Colonel from the Cuartel General (General Headquarters) in Buenos Aires snapped three color photographs of a glowing capsule-shaped flying object right over the capital city. He had gone home for lunch, and observing the object through his bedroom window called for his camera and snapped the three photographs from that location in front of his teenage son who witnessed the object and his father taking the pictures of it.

It was a dismal rainy day with a low densely overcast fairly dark sky. If fact the darkness of the afternoor may have been the reason for his having seen the strange flying object at all.

He had gone to his room at about 14:00 to change his clothes. Because it was exceptionally dark for that hour of the day, he went to the window and lifted the curtain and looked out. And there he was surprised to see an oblong orange light hovering over the ajacent apartment building. It was cylindrical in shape with rounded ends, and was glowing a bright orange color with an internal radiance it seemed. He lowered the curtain and continued dressing as he was late in getting away. He returned to the window for another look but the object was gone. He looked around for it, and in a few seconds saw it rising from behind the water tank on the roof of the other tall building, and then it descended some again and stopped and hovered in the air. About that time his son entered the room and seeing his father at the window went over and looked out also. They watched and discussed it for a short time, and the son thought it might be a UFO and suggested they take a picture of it. The Colonel got his camera and took the first picture, mostly to satisfy the son. After snapping the picture the light began to descend again, slowly until it disappeared behind the roof water tank once more. He set the camera down and finished dressing as the son watched out the window. In a few seconds the son called that the light was coming back up, and the Colonel took the camera back to the window again. The object was back above the building again, in about the same place, had the same luminous orange color, which was quite bright, and was beginning to move, so he quickly took the second picture. As it continued moving toward the east, the Colonel rolled the film and snapped a third picture. By then it was beginning to ascend, and the son called to his mother and his brother, who rushed to the room and saw the object too.

The Colonel didn't get to snap any more pictures in the efforts for all to see the object. The two sons insisted that this had to be a UFO, an opinion which the Colonel did not share at the time, as he did not believe in such things. While they were discussing this possibility, the orange light accelerated in a rising trajectory and flew away toward the east at such speed that they could not react fast enough to get another picture.

The ONIFE UFO research organization conducted an analysis of the original transparencies and concluded that they were authentic photographs of a UFO over the city of Buenos Aires.

The Officer was a War College graduate and an expert observer by anybody's standards. Needless to say, that family now believes that UFOs exist.

Guillermo Carlos Roncoroni of ONIFE

30 May 1975, 14:00, Buenos Aires, Argentina. An Army Colonel from the
Argentine General Staff Headquarters snapped these photographs from a
window of his bedroom in the city as he was changing clothes to go back
to work on a dark rainy afternoon. His two sons and wife also saw it.

30 May 1975, 14:00, Buenos Aires, Argentina. The third photograph of a
UFO observed right over the city of Buenos Aires by an Army Colonel
from General Staff Headquarters and his family from their home. This
enlargement shows that the radiant image has structure and form.

CREPY-EN-LAONNAISE, FRANCE
23 July 1975, 05:05

At 05:05 in the early morning of 23 July 1975, near Crepy-en-Laonnaise, Aisne Province of France, M. Jean Bonnet observed and photographed a self-radiant luminous orange colored capsule-shaped object flying at a relatively low altitude over the near countryside. This object was of the same shape, proportion, and almost the same orange color as a similar object photographed over Buenos Aires, Argentina on 30 May 1975. Bonnet knew nothing of the Argentine photos taken only a few weeks before the sighting in France.

Jean Sider

23 July 1975, 05:05, Crepy-en-Laonnaise, Aisne, France. This is the single color photograph of the radiant orange capsule-shaped UFO that was seen and captured on film by M. Jean Bonnet.

PEHUENCO BEACH, BsAs, ARGENTINA
9 May 1976, 18:30

At about 18:30 in the evening of 9 May 1976, Ms. Silvia Marie Weber was walking along Pehuenco Beach in Buenos Aires Province, about 60 kilometers northeast of Bahia Blanca, when she saw a number of people watching an unusual luminous yellow-orange capsule-shaped object flying slowly above the surf in the late afternoon sky. She went and got her camera and returned in time to snap one color photograph of the object before it flew away. The same or a very similar object was also observed at Tres Arroyos, 70 kilometers northeast of them only minutes later.

Guillermo Carlos Roncoroni

9 May 1976, 18:30, Pehuenco Beach, Buenos Aires, Argentina. Only this one color photograph was obtained by Ms. Silvia Marie Weber of the luminous yellow capsule-shaped object she and others watched as it was flying above the beach area.

At about 17:45 local time, on 28 May 1977, a Comodoro
in the Argentine Air Force, was driving his automobile
about 20 kilometers south of Alberti in the Province of
Buenos Aires, and had his son riding along with him. The
teenage boy first spotted a brightly luminous orange
colored capsule-shaped object flying slowly from north
to south beneath the low overcast clouds that late afternoon. The father tried to see the object pointed out
by his son also, and finally stopped the car to try to
see better. He got out with his camera, a Practika Pentacon 35mm hand held model with a 50mm lens attached. Now
they could clearly see a yellow-orange capsule-shaped
object moving along under the low clouds.

Before the father was able to take the first picture,
two brightly luminous yellow-white objects came out of
the larger capsule-shaped "mother-ship" and started to
fly around it. Then another came out and they all began
to fly behind the larger object. The Comodoro was trying
to snap pictures of this as fast as he could, but almost
immediately after launching the smaller craft, the larger ship disappeared into the clouds above followed in
quick order by the smaller objects.

The developed prints from the three color slides made
show the yellow-orange capsule-shaoed object and two of
the yellow-white "coolie-hat" shaped objects of smaller
size flying around the larger one as the whole gaggle
along under the overcast.

This sighting is remarkable because it is not often
that more than one object is captured in a UFO photo,
but in this case the "mother ship" was observed in the
process of launching smaller craft which then flew about
independently in the sky, and were actually photographed
together with the carrier. The objects were estimated to
be at least two kilometers away from the witnesses.

The Comodoro declines insists on complete anonymity
(his true name and address are on file) because of his
official position on active duty in the Argentine Air
Force.

Guillermo Carlos Roncoroni

160

28 May 1977, 17:45, Alberti, Argentina. These are the first two of the three color photographs of the orange luminous capsule-shaped carrier ship that launched three smaller yellow craft before ascending into the clouds with them. The smaller ones flew around the bigger one.

28 May 1977, 17:45, Alberti, Argentina. This is the third and last of the color photos of the luminous capsule-shaped "mother-ship" and its "brood" snapped by the Air Force Comodoro and his son.

BIG FLYING DISCS

In addition to the more commonly reported 30 to 60 foot diameter disc-shaped UFO craft, much larger sizes have been observed and photographed all over the world. For the purpose of this account, disc-shaped craft are not considered large until they exceed 100 feet in diameter. Even this is not large considering the fact that circular ships of 300 and even 500 feet diameter have been reported and photographed. This is a truely enormous flying object indeed. One such 500 foot diameter circular craft which was observed flying along a 1,000 mile track from central Brazil across Paraguay, Argentina and Chile, was described as a "Flying City" by many witnesses on the ground.

One of the first large circular flying objects photographed came from the South Atlantic towards the shore and over the beach at Barra da Tijuca near Sao Paulo, Brazil. It happened on 7 May 1952 while "O Cruziero reporter Joao Martins and newsphotographer Ed Keffel were on assignment at Barra da Tijuca to cover an official ground-breaking ceremony, and while they were waiting for the event ot begin, Martins suddenly spotted an object approaching in the air at high speed. It was then about 16:30 PM. He thought at first that it was an airplane. It looked like an airplane from that view (See the first picture), still there was something strange about it Martins realized. That plane was **flying sideways!** He shouted, "What the devil is that?" Keffel had his Rolliflex ready. Martins yelled, "Shoot, Keffel!" Ed Keffel aimed his loaded camera and got five excellent photographs in about 60 seconds, thus obtaining a most sensational photographic sequence of a Flying Disc.

Careful photogrammetric studies of each picture were conducted on the Keffel series. By calculating angles of elevation and trajectories it was possible to conclude that the object approached at about 1,600 feet altitude at just under a mile distance when the photographer began shooting pictures. It slowly descended as it approached the group and passed. After exhaustive study of these photographs the Brazilian Air Force released a positive statement that the pictures were genuine.

In response to an article published in the 10 May 1973

issue of "O Globo", a Rio de Janeiro newspaper, a gentleman wrote to Mre. Irina Granchi, a well known UFO investigator in the district, concerning a sighting of a UFO which he and a comapnion made in 1952. His letter is quoted as follows:

"Having read in "O Globo" a statement attributed to you in which you demonstrate your knowledge of, and interest in the so-called subject of flying saucers, I decided to write and tell you about an event I myself witnessed a long time ago in 1952.

"On a very clear sunny afternoon, I took a drive with my girlfriend, who is now my wife, to Barra da Tijuca... At about 15:00 hours we were heading for the Recreio dos Bandeirantes that runs parallel to the seafront there... When we reached Kilometer 6, some time later, an object caught my attention in the sky. It was very far off and looked metallic to us in the sunlight. At first we took it for a plane, but then, watching it more carefully, we saw that it was not moving. I stopped the car and we sat there and kept on watching it. After 2 or 3 minutes it suddenly took off at great speed, then disappeared behind some hills that stand at the beginning of the Barra at that point.

"Great was our surprise when, on the following week, we read a sensational report about a flying saucer having appeared at that same spot where we had seen that strange object. The article was illustrated by a series of photos, two of which showed the disc while it was flying toward the hill behind which we had seen it disappear. That event and the photographs coincide in date and hour with what we had seen." /s/_____(confidential)

In a postscript the writer stated, "I am a doctor and I should not approve of any publicity in my name", so it has been witheld.

That is one of the few cases of cross-verification of a UFO photographic event where neither party knew anything about the other at the time of the picture making.

From APRO Special Report Number 1, October 1961

The UFO debunkers went to great pains, unsuccessfully, to discredit this series of photos claiming hoax, and declaring that the shadow from a branch was in the wrong

164

position on the tree trunk. This was never successfully demonstrated, but carried a clear implication that the newsmen and the public officials at the ceremony and all the other witnesses present were in collusion to perpetrate such a hoax, and all this without any of the debunkers ever going to the scene and interviewing any of the other participants in the drama. One of them even devoted a section of his book to this ludicrous charge.

The next photographs of a huge disc-shaped UFO were taken on 9 August 1953 at Moscow, Idaho, when 5 black and white pictures were made. Witnesses, who decline identification, described and photographed a pinkish-white circular, disc-shaped object that hovered stationary in the sky about 1,000 feet above the ground. The estimated 200 foot diameter object, first seen in the north at about 21:30 moved slowly eastward and rose to about 8,000 feet altitude. A steady white light approached from below and to the east, and ascended and merged with the larger object. Four small white lights came from above and also merged with the larger luminous body hanging motionless in the sky. The photographer gave up observing at about 23:37 but the object remained in the sky until daylight, just before which it was seen as a small bright shiny object getting more distant.

FATE magazine, May 1954, p. 32 to 36

Witnesses at Fort Lamay in France reportedly observed and photographed a huge brilliantly luminous circular object in the night sky from 21:00 to 21:35 on 27 March 1955. This huge object was estimated to be about 300 feet in diameter by 120 feet thick from top to bottom.

From private personal correspondence.

The next, and more authenticated, case of such a large disc-shaped craft comes again from Brazil. In the late afternoon of 5 September 1955, Dr. Achilles Greco, a Brazilian Navy Officer, and a number of companions were returning from a recreational fishing trip on a small Brazilian Naval Boat, when they noticed a strange lenticular-shaped cloud moving independently of other cloud formations in the sky. It seemed to be following the Navy launch into the harbor at Santos. As they passed

Cabras Island, the very regular cloud shape began to change and they saw what appeared to be a solid object of some kind within it. The cloud substance was dissipating and drifting away and they could see a structured object of very large size inside. Dr. Greco prepared his camera and took one photograph of the strange flying object and its disappearing cloud cover. The object, formerly obscured by cloud matter, now appeared to be solid and metallic, and was estimated to be over 200 feet in diameter. The results of the investigation made by the Brazilian Navy have not been released.

August Roberts

Back here in the United States an even larger disc-shaped flying was photographed on 18 October 1957 near Winona, Missouri. In the early afternoon on that date an older gentleman, Mr. Tom O'Bannon, a grandfather, was returning from a birthday party for one of his grandchildren, and as he turned his old model car into his rural driveway, he noticed a huge, flat disc-shaped ship of some kind hovering nearly motionless only a few feet above the stubble field behind his house. As he watched, it began a slow rise and at the same time also started to move away. He quickly stopped the car and got out with an early style Polaroid Land camera he had been using at the party. He was able to get two black and white pictures before the object was gone. He could not get any more, even though the object was accelerating slowly, because of the necessity of "curing" the picture in the camera for 60 seconds before it could be removed. He did not take time to reset the focus and the light settings for the first shot, and it came out badly. He made up for this as that picture was curing, and the second photo was more clear even though the object was by now farther away. He immediately called the sheriff's office and they sent a deputy out to the house. He showed the photographs to the deputy, who took the good one and left. That one was never returned to Tom O'Bannon.

Mr. O'Bannon estimated the huge disc-shaped craft to be over 300 feet in diameter and a quarter to a half a mile away. It was a sort of brushed finish, metallic buff color, with a huge transparent dome of some kind on top. The old gentleman did not hear anything unusual and saw no flashes or lights. The ship seemed to have a very smoothe, clean finish with no seams or joining lines of any kind visible.

When word of this event got out, many people came to his door seeking more information and wanting to see, or wanted copies of the photographs made. At first he tried to comply but they overwhelmed him, and he began to refuse to see anyone. Visitors parked cars on his lawn, ran over his shrubs, trampled down his flowers trying to look into his windows and broke down his fence. He gave up and moved away. He refused to let his name be disclosed or to be further identified to any as long as he was alive, and did not want the exact location revealed because it might make a connection to him. He wanted no more of the public attention. I observed these restrictions for years. Finally, hearing that he had passed on, I published the picture and story in my UFO CONTACT FROM PLANET IARGA. A few months later I recieved a message from him through the daughter of my original contact, in which he reminded me of the restriction and that he felt quite well, but that little damage was done because he had moved again.

The best Polaroid picture, taken by the sheriff's deputy has never turned up since that time, and only the blurred our-of-focus first picture remains. This copy, poor as it is, was further damaged in being removed from a family album that had gotten rained on in a screened porch and pages stuck together.

From Mrs. Fanny Lowrey, a personal friend of O'Bannon

The next photo series of a huge disc-shaped UFO craft takes us back again to Brazil. On the afternoon of 24 April 1959, Sr. Helio Aguiar, a 32 year old statistician employed by a bank in Bahia, was test riding an Army Captain friend's new motorcycle down the coastal highway to Itapoan. As he was passing Piâta Beach in the Amaralina District, the cycle engine began to lug down and lose power. Then it quit and he rolled to a stop. As he put the kick-stand down and got off to look at the engine he noticed a silvery domed disc of immense size approaching from over the waters of the Atlantic Ocean there. It was shaped something like a Cardinal's hat (in the Catholic Church) with a number of windows or ports visible around the base of the high dome on top. On the under surface of the disc he saw some markings and four

167

hemispherical protrusions in a regular geometric formation. Looking around for help, he noticed a camera in a
case strapped to the luggage carrier on the back of the
machine. He quickly unstrapped it and opened the case.
He adjusted the settings and snapped four quick shots in
rapid succession as the object made a leisurely sweeping
turn from the sea over the surf toward the witness. Then
he began to feel a strange pressure in his brain, and a
state of progressive confusion overtook him. He felt
vaguely as though he were being ordered by somebody to
write something down. As he was winding the film for
the 4th picture, he lost all sense of what was happening
around him and fainted.

The next thing Aguiar knew, he was slumped over the
motorcycle and the UFO was gone. In his hand he held a
piece of paper bearing a message. It said: "Put an absolute stop to all atomic tests for warlike purposes. The
balance of the Universe is threatened. We shall remain
vigilent and ready to intervene." Some symbols followed.

As he tried to recall the experience, he remembered
that the craft was a darker silvery metallic color with
a somewhat luminous more orange colored, prominent dome.
The "windows" were small and square and looked more like
panels or ports running around the base of the dome.
There were three tubes or rib-like structures of some
kind running parallel from the dome to the edge of the
disc on one side, and it had four small hemi-spherical
protruberances on the underside, equally spaced 90 degrees to each other near the center of the bottom. Three
of the markings on the under surface of the disc flange
are faintly distinguishable in one of the photographs
made but they do not conform to any known symbol or language known to us today.

Although the object moved in a sweeping curve in its
flight path, it did not seem to employ aerodynamic lift
to remain aloft. When first seen, it was travelling edge
forward in a very steep bank, and then its position slowly changed so that in the last photo it is seen flying
dome forward in a maximum drag condition, with the full
area of the disc flat against its line of flight. Aguiar
did not see the craft depart.

SBEDV 24/25 Dec–Mar 1962

But that was not all there was to this case. Four and

a half years earlier, on the morning of 17 November 1954 Sr. Alberto Sanmartin was given an engraved tablet of violet colored stone flecked with bright yellow particles on which was engraved 9 symbols completely unknown to the witness, two of which appear on the underside of the flying disc photographed by Aguiar.

This remarkable stone tablet, flat and rectangular in shape, some 12 cm long by 4 cm wide by 2 cm thick, was given to Sanmartin by a UFOnaut dressed in a one-piece close-fitting coverall jump-suit made of fine material, and having no visible closures or pockets, who got out of a circular metallic flying craft of disc-form with a raised cupola on top, which with a quiet hum then ascended vertically at prodigious speed and disappeared into the clouds above.

The stone had faded to a greenish-gray color by the time Sanmartin got it to scientists to analyze. Several analyses were made but they all came out differently, as if to demonstrate that the technical nature of its formation was alien to our world.

This remarkable event took place at La Coruña, some distance from Piâta Beach. An entire book titled A PEDRA DO ESPACIO has been written in Portugese on the investigation and analysis of this mysterious extraterrestrial stone tablet. It is authored by Alberto Sanmartin and is only available in Portugese.

Disco Voador No. 2, p.18 to 20

What is even more amazing is the report that the U.S. Department of State obtained a copy of that piece of material held in Augiar's hand which had more symbols of unrecognizable form on it, and after inferred analysis, claimed they had broken the code and that the message contained a facitious greeting from Martian astronauts.

Then we have a report from half way around the world, in Japan, of a huge disc-shaped flying craft that approached an airline transport in flight with a full load of passengers. At 14:10 on 13 July 1962, Mr. Yusuke J. Matsumura, an officer of CBA (Cosmic Brotherhood Association), was riding an all Nippon Airways Viscount turbo-prop transport from Sapporo to Tokyo. ANA Flight 59 was cruising at 4,650 meters altitude when the immense disc-shaped craft approached from the left front of the airliner and passed beyond the wingtip and to the rear of

169

the transport. Matsumura had his camera in his lap and he raised it and snapped two good photographs of the slightly hazy or misty outlined UFO. He snapped his pictures at 1/1,000th second.

CBA Brothers, Vol. 2, No. 1, 1964, p. 88
Japanese Flying Saucer News, No. 3, 1966, p. 2 and 5

Three years later, in the same area, another photographer took pictures of a similar huge disc-shaped UFO in the sky passing an airliner in flight. At 13:10 on 27 September 1965, Mr. K. Kawai was riding an All Nippon Airways Boeing 727 jetliner near Mount Tsukuba, when he observed a gray hazy disc-shaped circular flying object of huge size flying there beyond the right wingtip of the air transport. It passed from front to rear on a slowly approaching trajectory and Kawai readied his camera and snapped three good photographs of this object before it passed. It was very similar to the one photographed by Matsumura nearly three years earlier.

Japanese Flying Saucer News, No. 11, 1965, p. 1
Japanese Flying Saucer News, Vol. 9, No. 3, 1966, p.23

Back here in the United States, on an undetermined day in January of 1967, Mr. James Bjornstad, a minister of youth at the Van Riper-Ellis Memorial Church in Fair Lawn, New Jersey, and research consultant at the Christian Research Institute of Wayne, New Jersey, observed and snapped one color photograph of a huge circular disc-shaped flying object. He was standing on the back porch of the Immaculate Conception Seminary, overlooking the rear yard of that institution in Mahwah, at about 13:00 local time, after his attention had been attracted to the object while driving on the street in front.

The color photograph shows a sharply defined structured object of a dark dull gray metallic color observed at an elevation of 30 to 40 degrees above the horizon in the sky. The object has a relatively thin disc-flange similar to the Piâta Beach UFO and a small dome-like cupola of top, also reminiscent of the Piâta craft, however in this case the dome looks to be of the same gray metallic color as the disc of the ship. This circular flying object is seen in a clear blue cloudless sky above some large bare-branched trees in the back garden of the seminary. It is shaped almost like the little wide-brimmed black hats worn by Cardinals in the Catholic Church. The disc is proportionately thin for its diameter, and of almost uniform thickness throughout, except for the dome. The rim appears almost as thick as the rest of the flange and seems to have a roll-contour to the edge. The dome is proportionately small, being in width about 1/3rd of the overall diameter of the disc, and raised in height above the upper surface about one thickness of the disc flange, proportionately smaller than on the Piâta UFO. The witness estimated the diameter to be quite large, indicating more than 100 feet. This sighting and photograph came at a time when there was a great deal of UFO activity in the eastern part of the United States. The object appeared to be silent and was not flashing any lights or leaving any kind of trail in its wake. The witness had never seen anything like this before. (From the files of August Roberts)

Photographs of the Unknown, Rickard-Kelly, p. 53
Saucer News, Vol. 15, No. 2, (Whole Number 72) Sum '68

Perhaps the largest disc-shaped flying craft ever photographed was the one that appeared over Bahia, Brazil, on 21 May 1972. This is not far from the location of the Piâta Beach photographs a few years earlier. It was at about 11:25 that Sunday afternoon that young Antonio Silva Menezes, then 18 years old, was on the rear patio of his home situated in the suburb, Liberdade de Salvador, in Bahia, trying to take a picture of his cat, when he saw a huge UFO in flight overhead, and managed to get one of the more spectacular pictures of this strange phenomenon. He was using a "Rio Kodak 400" camera with a Dakon lens set for photographing in bright sun. It was loaded with Agfa ASA 100 (21 DIN) film.

As he raised his eyes to observe the object, he could see that it was in and out among white cumulus clouds with bases at 1,500 feet and tops at 4,500 feet or more. The local meteorological service later confirmed cumuloform clouds in a broken layer (about 50% coverage) of that size at those altitudes. The huge circular object was moving at about the speed of a jet transport when first seen, but it was beginning to change direction as he aimed and snapped the photograph, steadying the camera on his knee in his sitting position. It changed from

171

horizontal to vertical flight and departed by ascending vertically at prodigious speed.

Antonio did not hear any sound of any kind coming from the big ship, and didn't see any flashing lights or any other effects. The craft looked to be oval at first, but as he saw more of it, it became quite apparent that it was circular and flattened, and of immense size. It was a dark silvery color, looked metallic, and was much brighter on top, possibly due to reflection of the sun high overhead at that time of day.

This great object was observed a little above mid-way between the bases and the tops of the white clouds, flying at an altitude conservatively estimated, based on the meteorological data, at about 3,000 feet. Re-enacting the sighting position and sitting posture of the photographer, Antonio's camera angle was found to be about 50 degrees above the horizon, and the distance was calculated to be about 3,900 feet. The UFO image measured 4 milimeters on the negative. Multiplying this by the distance to the object and dividing the result by the 3.5 focal length of the camera gives the flying object a stupendous diameter of just about 450 feet and an overall height from top to bottom of about 70 feet, almost nine stories! This is big enough to include a football field or 4 Boeing 747 Jumbo Jet Transports completely inclosed inside... a truely staggering size by any standard. The photographer checks out as exceptionally honest and sincere, well respected by his friends and neighbors, and is recognized for his personal integrity by his peers.

ONIFE Case No. 15, From Guillermo Carlos Roncoroni

Another large disc-shaped UFO was photographed near Waterdown, Ontario, Canada, at 13:30 on 18 March 1975. Amateur AstronomerPatric McCarthy (19) had gone to an abandoned quarry to photograph some wild birds there. He looked around the desolate area for some time and was walking back, "When suddenly I saw this massive circular object in the sky," he said. "I had been focusing my camera on a tree branch when I saw this thing like a big frisbe zig-zagging around above me. I just started snapping away as fast as I could."

He was having difficulty keeping the object in the viewfinder because it was "flitting about everywhere."

He estimated the size of the disc-shaped object to be about as large or larger than a DC-8 jetliner (about 100 feet) and travelling thousands of miles per hour. The quarry is just off Highway 5 from Waterdown.

The witness was using a 135mm telephoto lens and the object filled about 1/4th of the viewfinder. The film was taken to the Burlington SPECTATOR where the high school student told his story. The newspaper processed the film from his camera in their lab and found the developed film to show 4 picture frames of the object. In one frame the photographer missed the object completely. When the image was magnified 150 times, one frame showing the object in a side profile revealed two very thin rod-like protrusions from the bottom center of the dark circular craft. The ship appears dead black in all three frames showing its image, and it is tilted steeply, almost vertically to the right. Picture number 1 is the sharpest and the one which shows the rod-like appendages. Number 2 picture missed the object completely. Picture number 3 shows the object at about a 50 degree tilt and a view from a slightly upper angle. In photo number 4 the object is almost vertically inclined again with more of an angle view of the top. This view shows a somewhat asymetrical shape to the rim flange which has not been accounted for. A speck of dirt caught in the drying emulsion near the object marrs the third frame.

Mrs. Daisy Wilmot, living nearby, witnessed a similar UFO at about the same time. It hovered over a body of water about 500 yards from shore. She reported this object to police but gave little detail.

Exactly one week later, on 25 March 1975, Buddy Thomas (13) walking on Garth Srteet, a few blocks from his home in Burlington, Ontario, saw and photographed a 200 foot diameter silvery disc-shaped circular flying object hovering over the power lines on the east side of Garth.

Hamilton, Ontario SPECTATOR, 19 March 1975
Hamilton, Ontario SPECTATOR, 3 April 1975
UFO Quebec, No. 2, p. 15

The last large disc-shaped craft we have on record being photographed was sighted off the coast of South Herwang, West Indonesia, in November 1976. On an undetermined day of that month, at about 15:00 West Indonesian time, Mr. Tony Hartono of the ARCO Oil Company was taking pictures of the oil rig his company (Atlantic Rich-field Indonesia, a subsidiary of the Texas based oil company) was building in the offshore oilfields of those Indonesian waters. He used photographs to illustrate his progress report on the construction project. He was just leaving the rig in a launch and had one unexposed frame left in his camera as he stood on a platform facing the sea and the receeding oil rig. He was pondering what to shoot the last picture of in order to finish up the roll of film in the camera.

Suddenly his attention was attracted to a little dark speck, a distant object in the sky which was growing larger as it approached the oil drilling platform in the sea. At first he thought it was an airplane, but gave up that idea when he saw no recognizable detail for an airplane. It then became a yellowish color as it continued its approach and came quite near, then it began to accelerate, made a sharp turn, and quickly sped away while its glowing yellow color began to darken and take on a reddish hue. In the distance as it was leaving the area, it shot upwards vertically at a very high speed and went out of sight.

The photograph shows a quite large circular object, estimated to be 100 feet or more in diameter, of a dark reddish color with a thin reddish halo of a lighter co-lor surrounding the object. It is seen moving in the foreground of the picture at about a ten degree eleva-tion above the horizon. The drilling platform is seen in the background. The image shows some left to right dis-placemnent due to its motion while at the same time the drilling rig appears sharp and clear, indicating no pan-ning of the camera during this shot.

This same oil drilling platform has been visited sev-eral times by UFOs during the time period of this photo-graph, usually at night, when the visitors were seen as strange nochturnal lights of unknown source. No other photographs were made of these objects.

From J. Salatun, Air Vice Marshall, Indonesian AF

BIG FLYING DISCS

 7 May 52, 16:30, Barra da Tijuca, Brazil, Ed Keffel

 5 Sep 55, 17:00 Santos, Brazil, Dr. Achilles Greco

18 Oct 57   Winona, Missouri, Tom O'Bannon

24 Apr 59   Piâta Beach, Helio Aguiar

13 Jul 62, 14:10, Sapporo-Tokyo, Japan,Y.J. Matsumura

27 Sep 65, 13:10, Mount Tsukuba, Japan, K. Kawai

   Jan 67, 13:00, Mahwah, New Jersey, James Bjornstad

21 May 72, 11:25, Bahia, Brazil, Antonio Silva Menezes

18 Mar 75, 13:30, Waterdown, Ontario, Patric McCarthy

   Nov 76, 15:00, South Herwang, W. Ind., Tony Hartono

BARRA DA TIJUCA, BRAZIL
7 May 1952, 16:30

At about 16:30 in the afternoon of 7 May 1952, one of the big years for UFO activity, O'CRUZEIRO reporter Joao Martins and news photographer Ed Keffel on assignment at Barra da Tijuca near SAo Paulo, Brazil, waiting for some official groundbreaking ceremonies to begin, when Joao Martins suddenly spotted an unusual flying object approaching in the sky at high speed. It was coming in from over the south Atlantic towards shore, and over the area where they stood waiting with equipment ready to cover the political event. Martins noted that if it was an airplane, it seemed to be flying "sideways". "What the devil is that?" Martins inquired. Ed Keffel had his Rolliflex at hand and Martins yelled, "Shoot, Keffel". Keffel aimed his camera and started shooting as fast as he could roll the film, and he got five excellent photos of the object in 60 seconds, one of the most sensational sequences of a "Flying Disc" up to that time.

Photo number 1 shows the object at 1,600 feet altitude at a distance of 4,950 feet.

On picture number 2 the object has ascended to about 3,000 feet above sea level and has withdrawn to a further distance of about 6,500 feet.

In photos numbers 3, 4 and 5 the object is descending again with altitude estimates of 3,050, 2,350 and 1,950 respectively and distances of 3,950, 3,450 and 9,500 as it moved above. The Brazilian Air Force made exhaustive studies and photogrammetric analyses of these photos and released a positive statement that these photographs are genuine.

Of course all the officials and spectators at the public ground-breaking ceremony observed the phenomenon photographed that day by the newsmen. After the pictures were published in the local newspaper, there were many other witnesses who came forward to confirm the event. Even years later other confirmations were still coming in.

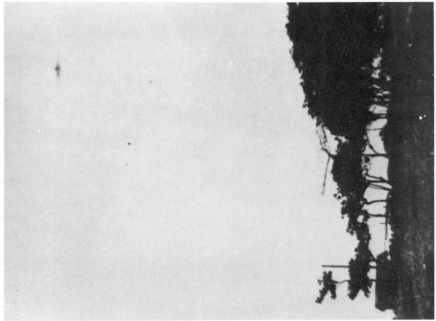

7 May 1952, 16:30, Barra da Tijuca, Brazil. Photographer Ed Keffel snapped pictures with his Rolliflex.

177

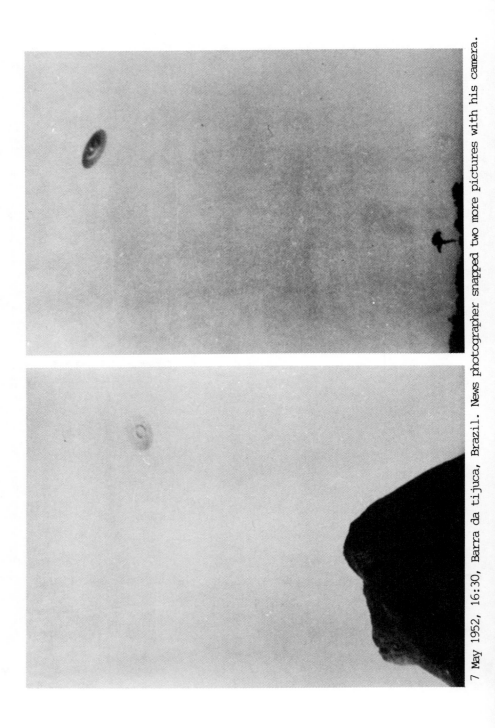

7 May 1952, 16:30, Barra da tijuca, Brazil. News photographer snapped two more pictures with his camera.

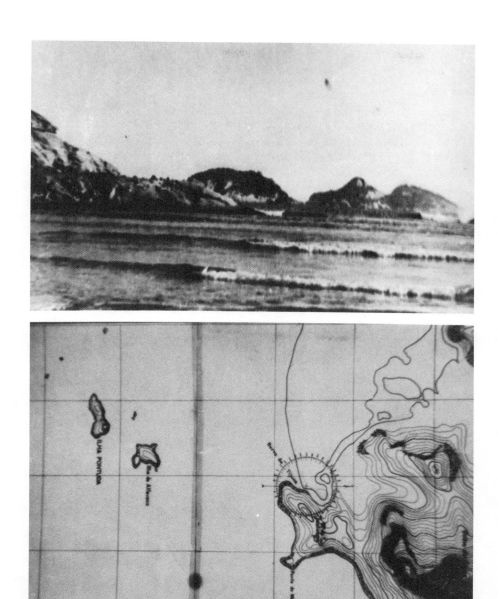

7 May 1952, 16:30, Barra da Tijuca, Brazil. The object begins a swift
low level departure back out to sea. A Map of the area shows the changes in course and trajectory taken by this flying object. It was seen
to disappear out over the water horizon.

SANTOS, BRAZIL
5 September 1955, 17:00

Late in the afternoon, about 17:00, on 5 September 1955,
a party of recreational fishermen including Dr. Achilles
Greco were returning to port in a small Brazilian Navy
Vessel after a day of deep sea fishing. Greco, a Naval
Officer, and his companions had been watching a strange
round, almost lenticular, cloud for some time as they
cruised toward port. This small very coherent cloud was
moving independently of other clouds in the sky that afternoon, and even seemed to be following the boat into
the harbor entrance at Santos. As they passed Cabras Island the "cloud" shape began to change and they observed
what appeared to be a solid object of some kind within
it. The cloud substance was dissipating and then began
to drift away. By now Greco had his camera ready and he
snapped one photograph of the structured disc-shaped object of huge size seen inside. The now revealed object
appeared solid and metallic, and was estimated to be 200
feet in diameter. A Navy investigation was not released.

5 September 1955, 17:00 Santos, Brazil. Dr. Achilles Greco's one photo.

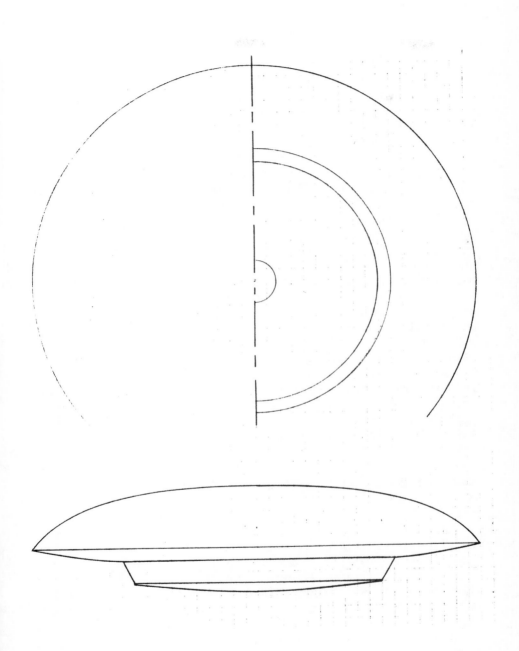

5 September 1955, 17:00 Santos, Brazil. Line drawing of the ship seen within the cloud over Cabras Island in Santos Harbor. As the cloud dissipated it the object was revealed.

WINONA MISSOURI
18 October 1957, Early Afternoon

In the early afternoon of 18 October 1957, an older
gentleman living near Winona, Missouri, was returning
from a birthday party for his grandchildren when he saw
a very large disc-shaped flying object. As Tom O'Bannon
turned his old car into the driveway of his rural
home, he spotted the huge circular, metallic craft low
in the air over a stubble field behind his house. It was
only a few feet above the ground, and as he watched, it
began to rise slowly and started to move away. He quickly stopped the car and got out with his old style Pola-
roid-Land camera he had been using at the party. He was
able to snap two black and white polaroid prints of the
strange machine before it was gone. He was unable to get
more, even though the object was moving slowly because
of the necessity of "curing" the picture in the camera
before it could be removed.

The first picture was quite out of focus because he
still had the settings for the party on the camera and
forgot to take time to change them for the first photo.
It did not come out well, but while that picture was
"curing" in the camera he did set it up for the next
picture and that one developed well, though the object
was much farther away by then.

He immediately called the Sheriff's Office and they
sent a deputy out to the house. O'Bannon showed the photographs to the Deputy who took the best one. It was not
returned and O'Bannon was never able to find out what it
was he photographed or where that picture went.

O'Bannon estimated that huge flat ship to be a stupendous 300 feet of more in diameter. Reconstruction of its
size from its position and width in the field later confirmed this. It was about a quarter of a mile from him
when he took the first picture or maybe a little more,
up to a half mile away. It had a sort of brushed metallic looking finish, not mirror bright, and it had
a wide flat transparent dome on top, that looked to be
about 1/4th the width of the ship. The witness did not
hear any sounds from the craft nor did he see any flashing lights or beacons. It appeared to have a very clean
unbroken surface with no seans or joining lines visible.

The remaining copy of this photograph in the hands of the witness, poor as it is, was further damaged in being removed from a family album which had gotten rained on inside a screen porch. The pages dried stuck together.

Two days later, on the 20th of October, the same man was occupied in trying to get a picture of a kitten and a puppy tusseling on the back patio, behind his house, when suddenly they scattered as though frightened from something. Turning to look over his shoulder O'Bannon saw another flying disc, smaller in size and thicker in proportion to width than the bigger one. This one was very low above the yard, below treetop level, and was rising and retracting some kind of understructure beneath it that may have been extended more before he saw it. It was about 15 to 20 feet in diameter, had a transparent dome on top and was of a brushed metallic silver color, quite bright. It was soundless and was rising quite rapidly. He was only able to turn and snap the one picture before it was too far away for another. That was at 16:00 in the afternoon, 30 miles east of Winona.

As he studied the developed polaroid print he now held in his hands he recalled seeing some circles on the under side of the larger one he had seen two days before, about nine of them grouped around the center on the bottom. He wondered if this craft could have come from the bigger one and occupied one of those positions. The more he thought about the more he became convinced that they were related and that he was guessing right.

He did not call the Sheriff this second time.

Mrs. Fanny Lowrey

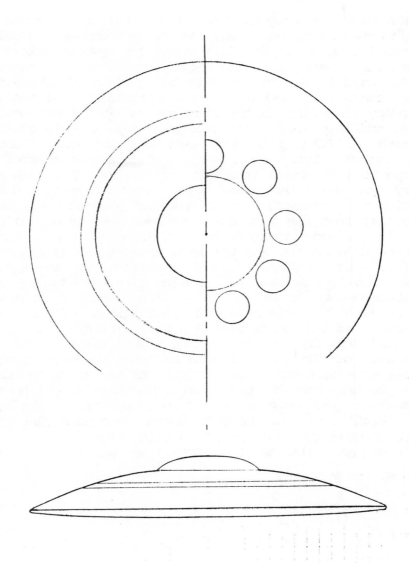

18 October 1957, Afternoon, 30 Miles easo of Winona, Missouri. This huge 300 foot diameter disc was discovered hovering only a few feet above a stubble field behind the photographer Tom O'Bannon's house.

184

18 October 1957, 30 miles east of Winona, Missouri. This first of two photos shows the big dim disc rising.

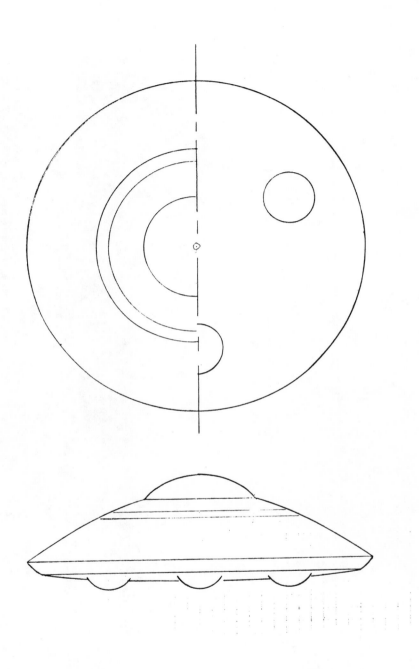

20 October 1957, 16:00, 30 miles east of Winona, Missouri. This is the
ship seen and photographed over the back patio two days after getting
the pictures of the big one over the stubble field behind the house.

186

20 October 1957, 16:00, 30 miles east of Winona, Missouri, Two days afterseeing the big craft behind his house, Tom O'Bannon was surprised to see this small one hovering over his back yard at the same place.

PIATA BEACH, BRAZIL
24 April 1959

On the afternoon of 24 April 1959, Helio Aguiar, a 32 year old statician employed by a banking firm in Bahia, Brazil, was riding an Army Captain friend's new motorcycle along the highway to Itapoan on a trial run to appreciate the Captain's recent purchase. As he came to the stretch of highway passing Piata Beach in the Amaralina district, the machine seemed to be losing power, and he looked around in dismay. Suddenly he noticed a big silvery-gray disc approaching in his direction from out over the water. It was shaped something like a cardinal's hat (Catholic Priest) with a number of "windows" or ports of some kind visible around a high raised dome on the top side. As it flew along it changed its pitch angle and could see the underside and that there were some strange markings or symbols on the bottom of the rim there. He could not make out what letters they were.

By this time the motorcycle had almost no power at all and the engine just quite. He put the kick-stand down and got off to ckeck it, noticing the Captain's camera strapped to the luggage carrier on the back of the machine. Looking back at the flying object he saw that it was much closer, then thinking of the camera he untied it and opened it up to take a picture of this strange airplane. He adjusted the settings and took four quick shots in rapid succession as the object made a sweeping turn from the sea toward him over the surf line.

Then he began to feel a strange pressure in his brain, and a state of progressive confusion overtook him. He felt vaguely as though instructed by somebody to write something down. As he was winding the film for the 4th picture he lost all sense of what was happening and does not remember snapping it.

The next thing Aguiar knew he was slumped over the motorcycle and the UFO was gone. In his hand he held a slip of paper with some words in his own handwriting on it. It said: "Put an absolute stop to all atomic tests for warlike purposes. The balance of the Universe is threatened. We shall remain vigilant and ready to intervene."

As he tried to recall what had happened, he remembered

that the craft was of a darker silvery metallic color with a lighter colored rounded dome on top, quite prominent. The "windows" were small and square and ran in a line around the base of the dome or cupola.

Besides that there were three tubes or rib-like structures of some kind running parallel straight from the dome to the rim edge of the disc on one side, and it had four small hemi-spherical protrusions on the underside, equally spaced around the middle near the center of the ship. The markings on the underside of the disc flange were clearly distinguishable with the naked eye, and are also faintly visible in the photographs taken but they do not conform to any known symbol or language familiar to us today.

Although the object executed a smoothly curving approach in its flight trajectory, it did not seem to be taking advantage of any aerodynamic lift to remain aloft in the course it pursued. When first seen it was traveling edge forward in a very steep bank to its left, and then its position changed to that seen in the last photo where it is traveling dome forward in a maximum drag condition, with the full area of the disc flat against the line of flight. Aguiar never saw it leave.

Four and a half years later, in a UFO contact case in another part of Brazil, a witness was given a small tablet of strange stone with 9 unusual symbols engraved on it, two of which are exactly like two of those photographed on the underside of this ship.

A little over six years later, at 04:30 AM on 12 July 1965, Mrs. Manual Fernandez, of the small village of Motosinhos, Portugal, saw a "cardinal's Hat-shaped" UFO hovering low over the trees near her home. It had a light orange dome on top with a darker brim. It leaned alternately from side to side, slightly, and then sped away without any apparent acceleration.

SBEDV 24/25 Dec - March 1962

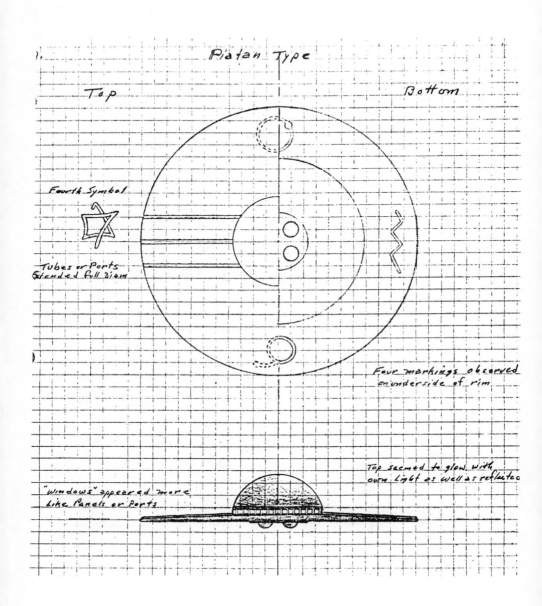

Piata Type

Top   *Bottom*

Fourth Symbol

Tubes or Ports
Extended Full Diam

Four markings observed
on underside of rim

Top seemed to glow with
own light as well as reflected

"windows" appeared more
like Panels or Ports

24 April 1959, afternoon, Piata Beach, Itapoan, Brazil. Line drawing of the huge craft from the sea. Note the symbols on the underside of the disc and the three ribs or tubes in the top surface. Four round hemispherical protrusions are seen near the center underneath.

190

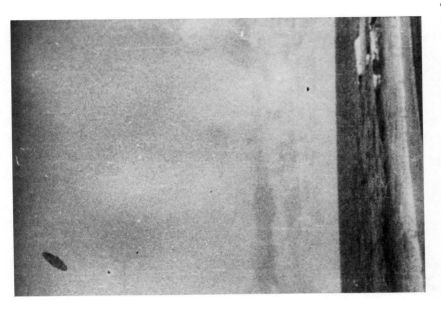

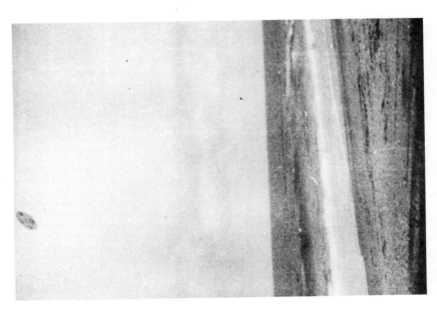

24 April 1959, Piata Beach, Itapoan, Brazil. Helio Aguiar began snapping photos when cycle engine stopped.

24 April 1959, Piata Beach, Itapoan, Brazil. After the last photos were snapped, Helio Aguiar fainted.

192

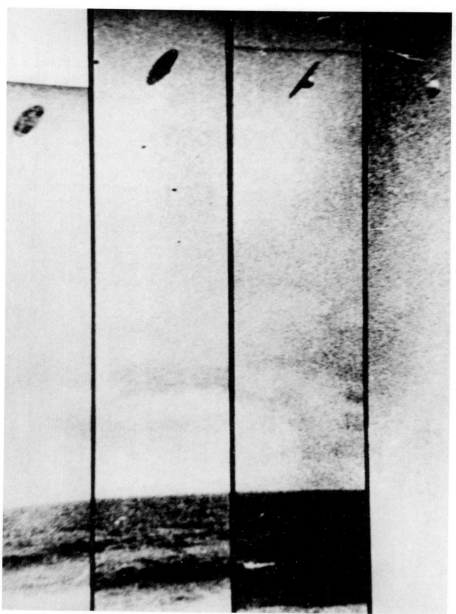

24 April 1959, Piata Beach, Itapoan, Brazil. The four photographs made by Helio Aguiar have been matched by surf line to show the actual trajectory of the approaching craft in the air. Aguiar did not know how he got the paper in his hand or where it came from. It had symbols.

SAPPORO—TOKYO, JAPAN
13 July 1962, 14:10

On 13 July 1962 Mr. Yusuke J. Matsumura, an officer of CBA (Cosmic Brotherhood Association) headquartered there in Yokohama, was riding an All Nippon Airways Viscount turboprop airliner enroute from Sapporo to Tokyo, ANA Flight 59, cruising at 4,650 meters altitude, when an immense disc-shaped craft approached from the left front of the transport and passed beyond the wingtip and to the rear of the airliner. Matsumura had been riding with his camera in his lap and he quickly raised it and managed to snap two good pictures of the slightly hazy and misty outlined UFO. He snapped his pictures at 1/1,000th second, in a bright cloudy sky. This craft was not unknown to Matsumura as he had seen this type before in his own personal UFO contacts, and was familiar with the occupants of these ships. The photos were made at 14:10.

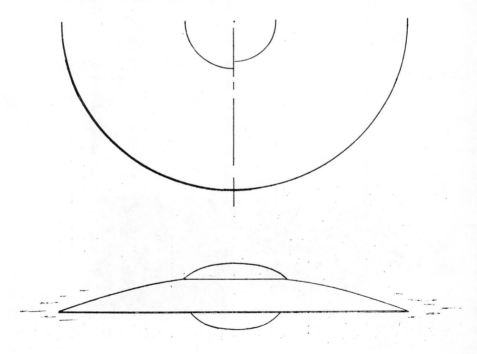

13 July 1962, 14:20, Sapporo—Tokyo Flight, Photograph, Y.J. Matsumura.

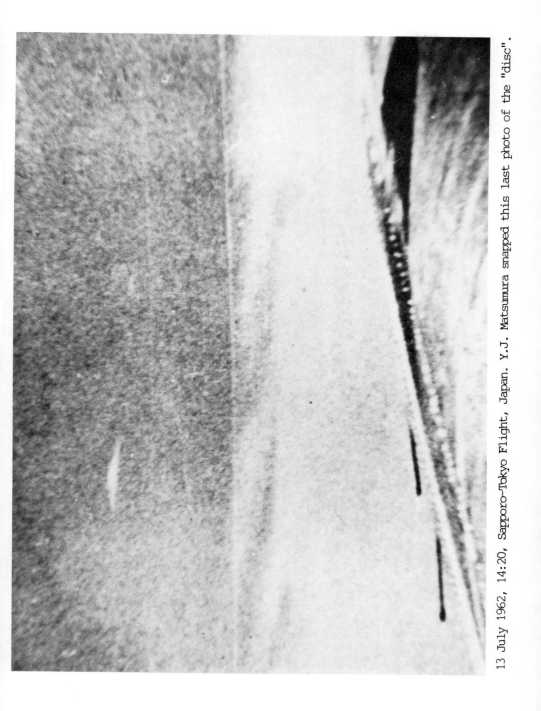

13 July 1962, 14:20, Sapporo-Tokyo Flight, Japan. Y.J. Matsumura snapped this last photo of the "disc".

MOUNT TSUKUBA, JAPAN
27 September 1965, 13:10

At 13:10 on 27 September 1965, Mr. K. Kawai, a local businessman, was riding on an All Nippon Airways Boeing 727 jetliner near Mount Tsukuba, when he suddenly saw a hazy gray circular disc-shaped craft of huge size flying off the right wingtip of the air transport. It passed from rear to front in a slowly approaching trajectory, and Kawai readied his camera and shot three pictures of this remarkable object before it passed and disappeared from view. The object seen in these photographs is very similar to the flying object photographed by Y.J. Matsumura on 13 July 1962. These photos are offered here for comparison.

27 September 1965, 13:10, Mt. Tsukuba, Japan. First photo by K. Kawai.

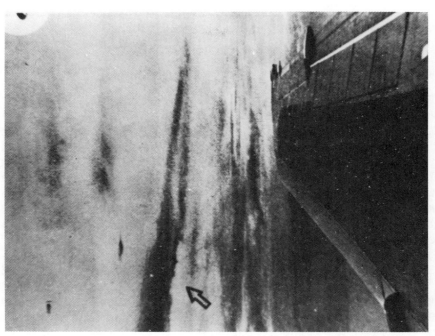

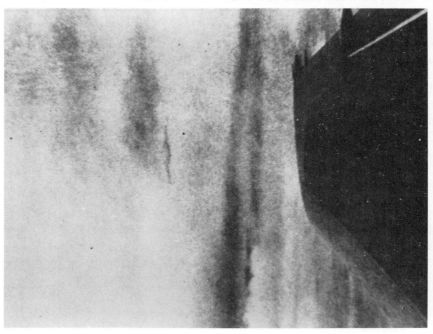

27 September 1965, 13:10, Mr. Tsukuba, Japan. 2nd and 3rd photos by K. Kawai through airliner window.

MAHWAH, NEW JERSEY
January 1967, 13:00

Right after lunch on an undetermined day in January of 1967, at around 1 o'clock pm., Mr. James Bjornstad, a Research Consultant at the Christian Research Institute in Wayne, New Jersey, and Minister of Youth at the Van Riper-Ellis Memorial Church in Fairlawn, New Jersey, and former student at the New York Theological Seminary in New York, was driving in the vicinity of the Immaculate Conception Seminary in Mahwah when his attention was attracted to an something flying in the sky. Through the trees along the street he could see a dull dark gray object sitting almost motionless in the sky beyond

Stopping the car in front of the Seminary Bjornstad got out with his Japanese brand 35mm hand camera loaded with outdoor color film, and walked through to a better vantage point, adjusted the distance setting to infinity and snapped one picture of the strange flying machine.

Shortly after he snapped the color photograph, the circular object shot off instantly and went out of sight, before he could get another. The witness estimated the diameter to be quite large.

When the photographer received the developed roll of film and prints back, he saw that the picture had come out very clear and sharp. He really didn't think much about it at the time because he was not interested in UFOs, and didn't believe in them anyway. But this event roused his interest the more he thought about it, and he began a research project on UFOs for the Christian Research Institute for a booklet on UFOs.

This sighting followed by one year, the spectacular series of night sightings, and photographs of the UFO at Wanaque Reservoir, very near here.

Bjornstad, who lives at 7 - 13 River Road, Fair Lawn, New Jersey 07410, prepared a signed affidavit witnessed by Paul Blattner, Jr., and August C. Roberts.

August C. Roberts

198

Last January 1967, I was driving in the area of the Immaculate Conception Seminary in Mahwah, New Jersey around 1 pm. Through the trees, I spotted a dark gray object sitting in the sky. I had a Japanese brand 35 mm camera with with outdoor color film in it. I set the distance at infinity and snapped a picture of it. Shortly after I had taken the picture of it, it shot off instantaneously. When I had the roll of film developed, the picture came out very clear, but I never thought much about it, because I didn't believe in UFO's. Now I have been researching a project for the Christian Research Institute on UFO's for a booklet, and I remembered the photo I had taken.

I am a Research Consultant at the Christian Research Institute in Wayne, New Jersey. I am also Minister of Youth at the Van Riper Ellis Memorial Church in Fair Lawn, New Jersey. I attend school at New York Theological Seminary in New York. My address is 7 - 13 River Road, Fair Lawn, New Jersey 07410

* James Bjornstad

James Bjornstad

3/21/68 Paul F. Blattner, Jr.

August C. Roberts

January 1967, Mahwah, New Jersey. An Affidavit was prepared by James Bjornstad for August Roberts on 21 March 1968 after Roberts had made his investigation of the case and and was going to present it on a radio talk-show in the New Jersey area.

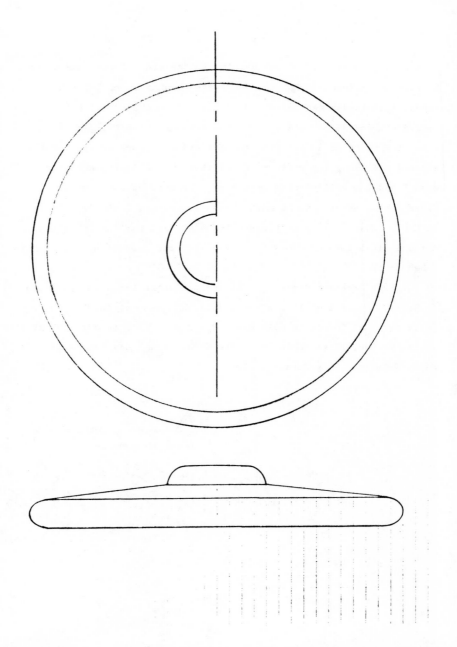

January 1967, Mahwah, New Jersey. Line Drawing of the huge circular object photographed by Mr. James Bjornstad as it flew over the rear grounds of the Immaculate Conception Seminary in Mahwah. The object was of a dull dark gray color and quite flat in appearance.

200

January 1967, 13:00, Mahwah, New Jersey. This single color photo was made by James Bjornstad by Seminary.

BAHIA, BRAZIL
21 May 1972, 11:25

One of the largest disc-shaped flying objects ever to be photographed was the one that appeared over Bahia, Brazil, on 21 May 1972. At about 11:25 that sunday morning, young Antonio Silva Menezes, then 18 years of age, was crouched on the rear patio of his home in the suburb Liberdade de Salvador in Bahia, trying to take a picture of his cat, when he noticed the huge circular object flying in the clouds overhead. He shifted his attention and, sitting down and steadying his elbow and camera hand on one raised knee, managed to get one of the more spectacular photographs of this strange phenomenon. He was using a "Rio Kodak 400" camera with a Dakon lens set for photographing in bright sun. It was loaded with Agfa ASA 100 (21 DIN) film.

This immense object was flying in and out of cumulous clouds with bases at about 1,500 feet and tops at the time at about 4,500 feet or more. The local meteorological service later confirmed cumuloform clouds in a broken layer (about 50% coverage) of that size at those altitudes. This huge object was moving at about the forward speed of a jet transport at cruise when first seen, but was beginning to change direction as he snapped the photograph. The craft changed from horizontal to vertical flight and departed by ascending vertically at prodigious speed.

Antonio did not hear any sound of any kind coming from the big ship, and didn't see any flashing lights and no other effects of any kind. The craft looked oval at first but as he saw more of it it became quite apparent that it was circular and flattened, and of truely gigantic dimensions. It was a dark silvery-gray color, looked metallic, and seemed to be much brighter on top, possibly due to reflection of the sun high overhead at that time of day.

The great object was observed a little above mid-way between the bases and the tops of the white clouds, at an altitude conservatively estimated, based on meteorological data, at about 3,000 feet. re-enacting the sighting position and posture of the photographer, Antonio's camera angle was found to be about 50 degrees above the horizon, and the distance was calculated to be about 3,900 feet. The object image measured 4 milimeters on the negative. Multiplying this by the distance and then dividing the result by the 3.5 focal length of the camera gives the UFO an object diameter of just about 450 feet and a height of about 70 feet. This is big enough to include a football field or 4 Boeing 747 Jumbo Jet transports completely enclosed inside... a truely vast craft by any standard.

The photographer checks out as exceptionally honest and sincere, well respected, and is recognized for his personal integrity by his friends and acquaintences.

Guillermo Carlos Roncoroni

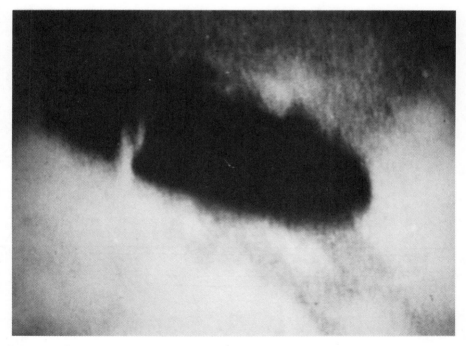

21 May 1972, 11:25, Bahia, Brazil. This is the single photograph of an immense circular flying object in the clouds above the city of Bahia in Brazil. It was calculated to be over 400 feet in diameter.

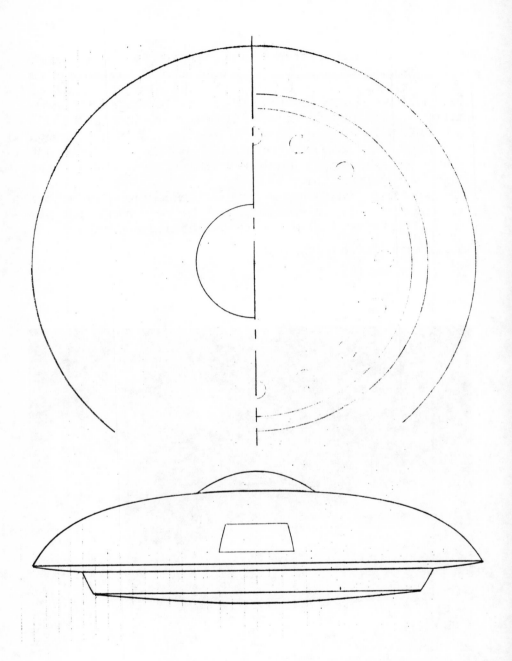

21 May 1972, 11:25, Bahia, Brazil. Line drawing of the huge ship seen and photographed by Antonio Silva Menezes, 18 years old, from the rear patio of his home in Liberdade de Salvador suburb in Bahia. It was flying about 3,000 feet above the ground when photographed.

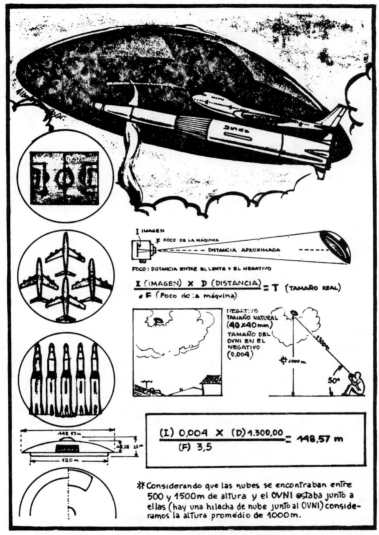

21 May 1972, 11:25, Bahia, Brazil. This sketch shows the relative size of this stupendous craft when compared with a football field as well as with four Boeing 747 Jumbojets that could be parked inside of it. Note also that it was 70' (almost 9 stories) from top to bottom.

205

WATERDOWN, ONTARIO, CANADA
18 March 1975, 13:30

A large disc-shaped UFO was photographed in the vicinity of Waterdown, Ontario, at 13:30 on 18 March 1975.
Amature astronomer Patric McCarthy, 19 years old, had
gone to an abandoned quarry to try to photograph some
wild birds there. He had poked around in the desolate
area for some time and was just starting to walk back
when, "Suddenly I saw this massive circular object in
the sky," he said. "I had been focusing my camera on a
tree branch when I saw this thing like a frisbe zig-zagging around above me. I just started snapping away as
fast as I could."
He was having difficulty keeping the object in the
viewfinder because it was "flitting" about everywhere.
He estimated the size of the disc-shaped object to be
about as large or larger than a DC-8 jetliner (about 100
feet) and traveling thousands of miles per hour. The
quarry is just off Highway 5 from Waterdown.
The object filled about 1/4th of the viewing area as
seen through the 135mm telephoto lens on the camera. The
hat-shaped object pitched about and changed angles and
elevations rapidly as the witness tried to hold it in
his viewfinder. The object moved so rapidly he could not
get more pictures. The exposed film was taken to the
Burlington SPECTATOR where the high school student told
his story. The newspaper processed the film in their own
lab and and found the developed negatives to show four
picture frames of the object sequence. In one frame the
photographer had missed the object completely. When the
image was magnified 150 times, one frame showing the UFO
in profile revealed two very thin rod-like protrusions
from the bottom center of the craft. The craft appears
dead black in all three frames showing the image, and it
is tilted steeply, almost vertically to the right.
Picture #1 is the sharpest and the one which shows the
rod-like appendages. In picture #2 the object was missed
completely. Picture #3 shows the object at about a 50
degree tilt and a view from a slightly upper angle. In
photo #4 the object is almost vertically inclined again
with more of an angle view of the top. This view myster-
iously shows a somewhat asymetrical shape to the rim

flange which has not been accounted for. A speck of dirt caught in the drying emulsion near the object marrs the third frame.

A degree of confirmation came when Mrs. Daisy Wilmot, from a point nearby witnessed the same or a very similar UFO at about the same time on that day. It hovered over a body of water about 500 yards from shore.

More confirmation came one week later, on 25 March 1975, when Buddy Thomas (13) walking on Garth Street, a few blocks from his home in Burlington, Ontario, saw and photographed a 200 foot diameter silvery disc-shaped circular craft hovering over the power lines on the east side of Garth. This is in the same general area as the quarry site.

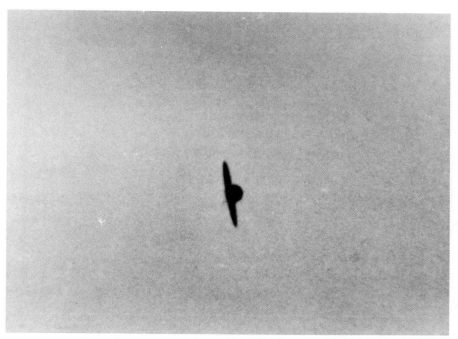

18 March 1975, 13:30, Waterdown, Ontario, Canada. This is the first and best of the three images captures in the four-shot sequence. Notice the antenna-like protrusions from the under surface of the big craft. A featureless black object was recorded in all three image frames.

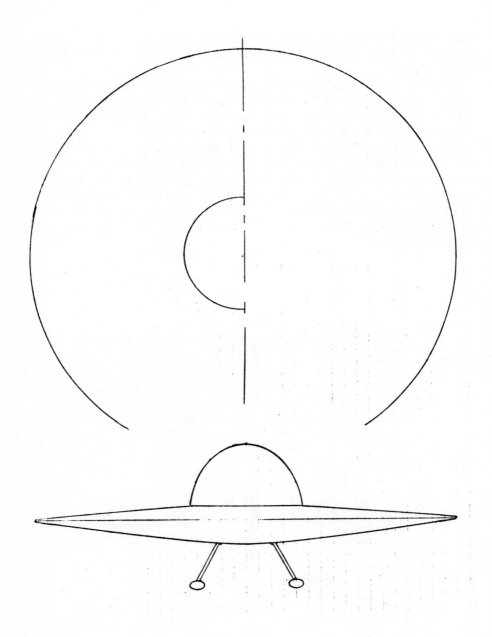

18 March 1975, 13:30, Waterdown, Ontario, Canada. Line Drawing of the
huge circular craft observed and photographed over the old quarry by
young Patric McCarthy, 19, as he was looking for a certain bird he
wanted to photograph that day.

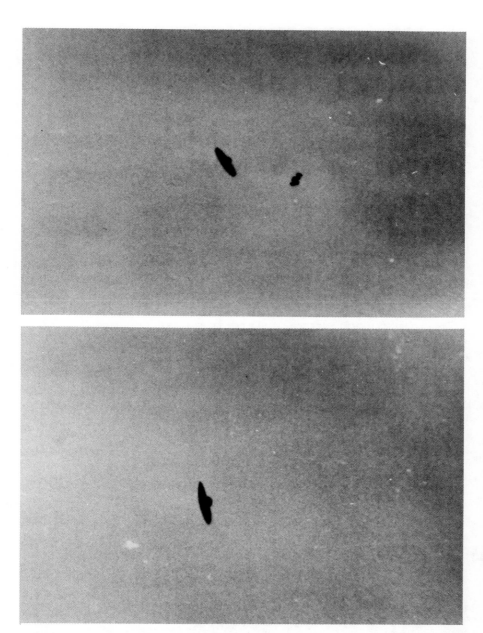

18 March 1975, 13:30, Waterdown, Ontario, Canada. Patric McCarthy (19)
snapped these last two pictures of the huge object that was "flitting"
around so wildly that he actually missed it in picture number two in
this four-shot sequence. The first picture was the clearest of all.

SOUTH HERWANG, INDONESIA
November 1976

On an undetermined day in November 1976, at near 15:00 West Indonesian Time, Mr. Tony Hartono, an engineer, had taken photographs of the off-shore oil rig his company ARCO Indonesia was building in order to illustrate his progress report. He had one frame left and was standing on a platform facing the sea, wondering what else he could shoot the last frame of to finish the film roll. Suddenly his attention was attracted to a little dark speck in the sky which was growing larger as it approached. It became a yellowish color as it continued its approach and came quite near the launch he was in.

Then it began to accelerate, made a sharp turn and sped rapidly away, while its glowing yellow color turned to a reddish hue. In the distance it shot up vertically at very high speed and went out of sight above.

The photograph shows a larg circular object of a dark reddish color with a thin reddish halo of lighter color surrounding it at the middle. The object is moving from left to right with the drilling rig in the background.

The image shows some left to right displacement due to its motion while the rig is sharp and clear, indicating no panning of the camera while the shutter was open.

November 1976, 15:00, Off South Herwang Coast, Indonesia. Tony Hartono.

CONCLUSIONS

From the foregoing it is immediately apparent that the nomenclature "Flying Saucer" is a term deficient in description and actually a misnomer for all but a fractional class of the total phenomenon. For this reason we prefer to use the term UFO which automatically, by definition, excludes those objects identified as mundane things, misperceptions and outright hoaxes.

We have found that these mysterious UFOs come in all shapes and sizes, from discs; small and large, shiny and flat, light and dark, big and small, fat and thin, hi-domed to no-domed and double-domed; to cylinders, also of all sizes and types, big and small, light and dark, slender and fat, with truncated ends and with pointed ends; and that this great variety of objects is seen under all kinds of conditions, in daylight and darkness, reflective and dull, radiantly luminous and light absorbing, in clear sky and in clouds, and sometimes even generating their own kind of mist or cloud cover.

The larger sizes have been seen and photographed launching and recovering smaller objects apparently carried inside the ship, which fly around independently. Sometimes there is a variety of types of craft involved.

These strange flying objects are seen over all parts of the world, in all temperatures and climates, and by all classes and races of people, often not in ready contact with anyone else who has seen something similar. Frequently each witness believes himself to be the only percipient after his own experience, and is not overly willing to risk ridicule by widely reporting his event.

We have long felt that for every UFO photo case that comes to our attention there are ten that do not, and we are aware of five times the number of photo cases presented here in each category.

That leaves a stupendous amount of information untapped at our level of society. We are aware that other levels of investigation have many times the number of UFO photo cases available to us, most of which have not been reported publicly anywhere.

This being the case, we insist that the UFO phenomenon is in fact REAL, and that photographs have been made. We feel that what we have presented here will stand all testing, and will never be successfully disproved. We invite any and all to proceed, with the data we have offered, and attempt to find where we failed to detect the flaw that would disprove any of these cases. We welcome any corrections to the data we have offered here.

We note that of all the debunkers who claim that these photographs could be easily duplicated with little real effort, not one has ever done so. Now is a good time to start...

UFO PHOTO ARCHIVES
P.O. Box 17206
Tucson, Arizona 85710
U. S. A.

UFO PHOTO CATALOG

This brief catalog is provided in chronoligical order by date and time for best and easiest use. We have been careful to include here all of the data factors known in each case, which would lend to classification, such as the following, when known:

1. Date
2. Time
3. Place
4. Photographer
5. What he was doing
6. How discovered
7. What it was doing
8. Number of witnesses
9. Number of Objects
10. Kind (shape, style)
11. Form (structured, wispy, shrouded)
12. Type (luminous, radiant, reflective, dark)
13. Color
14. Movement
15. Sound
16. Number of photographs
17. How object departed
18. Camera
19. Duration of observation
20. Source

CATALOGUE OF UFO PHOTOGRAPHIC REPORTS, WORLDWIDE

With the advent of modern home computer technology it has now become possible to process data in a big way as a hobby interest at home. We need more sophisticated analysis of the data available to rationalize the various factors in order to more effectively study what we have going on all around us. There has long been a need for more statistical analysis and for classification studies and trends. With that in mind we have decided to publish our file of UFO photographic reports for those who are interested in establishing their own database on this subject.

This appendix is intended to serve as a reference catalogue of UFO photo reports. Every effort has been made to include all the UFO cases reported or known of where the unknown flying object was photographed. While the search has been diligent and broad in scope, the compilers immediately recognize the existence of UFO photographic cases not yet reported. We are therefore planning a further supplement for a future volume to pick up new and missed reports, and to correct those already published.

These reports are listed in chronological order by date and time, and show the place and photographer's name, number of photographs, a brief summary of the report, and a source reference for additional information on the photographs.

Some deletions have been made in these reports at the specific request of the photographers or owners concerned. Many such individuals want no publicity, and do not want to be interviewed and interrogated, and they refuse to give up their original negatives or prints. We have agreed to withold as requested in order to be able to include what data we could so as not to lose the pictures from the catalogue. We have verified the data shown to the best of our ability but have at the same time committed ourselves to respect the confidences imposed.

In other cases omissions have had to be accepted for lack of data. Again we have decided to accept the omissions and keep the report in rather than to leave it out altogether.

Where days of a month are not available the report is listed at the end of that month. Where months are not known, the report is likewise shown at the end of that year. Where the year is not known, the best estimate of the approximate year will be used in order to keep the whole catalogue in context.

New information and corrections may be mailed directly to this publisher for updating.

While great pains have been taken to verify that these objects photographed are truely unknown and not hoaxes or misidentifications, we have had to rely on our information available and our best judgement. We have eliminated all known hoaxes and true misidentifications where the facts are known to us, however we are quick to agree that where the object is truely unknown we can be deceived. We therefore offer no rateing system or test for reliability and stand on the basis that the objects photographed and reported herein are still unknown to us. We acknowledge the possibility that some knowns may have escaped our detection and are included here. For those we apologize and ask to be corrected.

We offer no photographs for sale and accept no responsibility for transactions with photo sources.

While we have scanned all available material, we know that we have missed a number of photographs reported, and others that are still in the hands of original witnesses and have never been reported. We desire to stimulate submission of these to one of the UFO study groups or directly to us so that they may be worked into the system and become available to serious researchers. Perhaps one of these holds the key to resolution of this profound mystery.

A key to reading the IRC Printout codes was published as Appendix II in volume I of this series.

Escalation of the mini-wave of UFO sightings over the nation's capitol buildings was just beginning to be felt. UFOs had appeared in the
prohibited airspace twice the night before, easily penetrating all
defense nets and operating with total immunity. Waves of defense interceptor aircraft sent up to drive them off were completely ineffec-
tive, but they did get radar and gun-camera photos of the intruders.

. . . . .

20 July 1952, Washington D.C., 11:40 PM to 06:00 AM
A second massive fly-over of the U.S. Capitol occurred. This time 19
UFOs were reported, flying in formations of 3 and 9 ships. These craft
had bright white lights on two sides with a structured form in between
and the lights blinked in separate sequence at times and then again
they would blink together.
Canadian UFO Report, Vol. 2, No. 8, p 12-16

26 July 1952, Washington D.C., 22:30
Official USAF gun-camera film (16mm) was shot from an F-94 interceptor
fighter piloted by Lt. William Patterson from Langley AFB, which was
sent up to check out a huge luminous orange sphere operating in the
prohibited airspace over the capitol. Mr. Albert Chop, the Official
UFO Press Representative for the Air Force; Maj. Dewey Fournet, the
Pentagon Liaison Officer with Project Bluebook, and Lt. Holcomb, an
electronics expert working with the Air Force Directorate of Intelligence, watched the exercise in the ARTC Radar room at Washington International Airport for 2 hours.
A confidential personal report

27 July 1952, Lake Michigan, 21:40
Capt Ned Baker, commanding a flight of three F-94 interceptor fighter
aircraft, was ordered to intercept and check out a UFO that was changing colors from red to green to white. He had it on his radar, which
showed it at a distance of 65 kilometers, moving at 1,000 kmh at 6,000
feet altitude. He pursued it for 20 minutes and reportedly got gun-
camera film of the unknown maching.
A confidential report

28 July 1952, Jersey City, New Jersey, 00:01
A UFO was reportedly photographed by an unidentified witness. No other
details are available.
IRC Printout. source E 9V 0734Q

28 July 1952, New York City, New York, 00:11
Mr. August C. Roberts on official Skywatch duty snapped an official
Civil Defense photograph of a solid-looking metallic-looking flying
object with a big orange light. It was circular or disc-shaped and had
a reddish-brown edge. It approached the Skywatch tower from the direction of the Empire State Building in downtown New York.
August C. Roberts

29 July 1952, Passiac, New Jersey, 16:30
Mr. George Stock, working on a lawnmower in the yard of his home in
Passiac, looked up and saw a high-domed circular object flying toward
him. He ran for his camera and got 5 very clear sharp black and white
photographs of the solid-looking disc-shaped craft having a transparent dome on the top. It continued its approach and passed above the
ridge-line of his house and out over the back yard and away. It traveled slowly about 200 feet above the ground in a steady motion. The
object was about 25feet in diameter and had a metallic color and finish. It slowed and hovered momentarily, then accelerated and flew out
of sight over the horizon.
August C. Roberts

29 July 1952, Miami, Florida, 12:35
Mr. Ralph Mayer shot several feet of 16mm movie film of a 30 to 50
foot luminous spheroid moving at an estimated 7,550 mph in the night
sky over Florida.
SAGA UFO Report, July 1977 (Computer analysis by GSW)

29 July 1952, Osceola, Wisconsin
A 16mm movie of a UFO was reportedly taken by an unidentified witness.
No other details are available.
From a confidential source

29 July 1952, Washington, D.C.
A line of luminous lens-shaped objects were reportedly photographed
flying over the dome of the United States Capitol. Some critics argue
that these images are lens flares from the lights on the Capitol step.
M. Jean Sider

31 July 1952, Near Milan, Italy, 09:30
Sgn. Gampiere Monguzzi and his wife reportedly observed and made 7
black and white pictures of a disc-shaped UFO landed in the snow of
Cherchen Glacier near Bernina Pass. An occupant is seen outside of the
landed craft in two of the photographs. Some critics claim that the
pictures were made with table-top models, but Ms. Lou Zinsstag, a vet-

eran UFO researcher from Switzerland who knows Monguzzi and his wife personally, claims that she is certain the photos are legitimate unknowns and not models. She has the original negatives. Herr Adolf Schneider studied these photos at great length, and went to the actual scene where he took measurements and made calculations, and concluded that the pictures were probably real. He published an extensive report on his investigations. The Monguzzi camera was a Retina I manufactured by Kodak. It used a Schneider 1/3.5 lens set at f8 and 1/500th second for the pictures obtained. It was loaded with Ferrania 21 DIN film.
Personal Lou Zinsstag
Flying Saucer Review, Sept-Oct 1958, p 1-4
THE INTELLIGENT MAN'S GUIDE TO FLYING SAUCERS, T.M. Wright, p 101-104
SVELATO IL MISTERO DEI DISCHI VOLANTI, p 38

July 1952, Kutstown, Pennsylvania
A dark blurred spheroid was photographed in flight by an unidentified witness. No other details are available. Two black and white photographs were published. The witness was later identified as John Mitti.
Dell Flying Saucers, UFO Reports, No. 1, p 58
True Flying Saucers & UFOs Quarterly, No. 13, Spring 1979, p 54

July 1952, New Zealand
A UFO was observed flying through the sky in a jerky motion and was photographed by Mr. A. Roberts.
A confidential source

July 1952, Seattle Washington
A UFO was reportedly photographed by a witness identified only as Shankland. No other details are available.
IRC Printout, source 5N52GV

1 August 1952, Wright-Patterson AFB, Dayton, Ohio, 10:55
F-86 pilots, Lts. James Smith and Donald Hemer, pursued a faint dark disc-shaped object from 9,150 meters up to 12,000 meters (36,000 feet) and supposedly shot 16mm gun-camera photos of the target.
FLYING SAUCERS FROM OUTER SPACE, Donald Keyhoe, p 107-108
True, December 1952
THE UFO EVIDENCE, NICAP, p 88
Hartford, Connecticut COURANT, 2 Aug 52

Summer 1952, Chicago, Illinois
Mr. George Charney reportedly photographed a football-shaped UFO in the sky over the windy city. No other details are available.
FLYING SAUCERS UNCENSORED, Harold T. Wilkins

5 August 1952, Mayaguez, Puerto Rico
A friend of Garcia Mendez snapped photographs of 3 large UFOs flying
in formation toward Mayaguez. The photos were given to Ramey Air Force
Base Intelligence. They were never released by the Sir Force, and were
never returned, Their whereabouts today is unknown.
SAGA UFO Report, August 1977, p 6

5 August 1952, San Juan, Puerto Rico, 19:30-20:00
Three large disc-shaped UFOs were photographed flying horizontally
towards Mayaguez. One was larger than the other two. All were a rosey-
yellow in color. The photographs, delivered to Air Force Authorities
for examination were never returned. This is believed to be another
report on the photos described above.
PLATILLOS VOLADORES SOBRE VENEZUELA, Horacio Ganteaume, p 82

6 August 1952, Lima-Panama, 05:30
A UFO was reported photographed by a witness identified only as Quinn
riding on an airliner in flight. No other details are available.
IRC Printout, source J 600 54FS

13 August 1952, Caracas, Venezuela, 17:30
Photographer Jesus Delgado and a class of graduates observed a round
UFO over Catia. It was 8-10 kilometers distant, traveling north to
south, and was leaving a strange whitish trail behind it. The object
hovered momentarily and maneuvered beside a cumulo-nimbus cloud. It
finally ascended at incredible velocity toward the west.
"La Esfera" Daily, 23 October 1952
PLATILLOS VOLADORES SOBRE VENEZUELA, Horacio Ganteaume, p 95

August 1952, Wright Field, Dayton, Ohio
Two Air Force F-94 jet interceptor aircraft with gun-cameras loaded
were vectored in on a radar blip for identification. Both pilots saw
the object and one locked on with his air intercept equipment. As he
reached his maximum altitude, with the object getting away, he trig-
gered his gun-camera and captured the object on 16mm movie film.
Memo for the Director of Intelligence (sanitized copy)
Flying Saucer Review, August 1952

2 September 1952, The Netherlands
A very large bright round self-luminous flying object was photographed
hovering in the air above a factory. Radiated light reflected from the
rooftops of the building below seem to lend validity to this photo.
UFOs, A PICTORIAL HISTORY, Knight, p 59

19 September 1952, Operation "Mainbrace", North Sea, 16:00
Mr. Wallace Litwin from the newsreporters pool aboard the U.S. Aircraft Carrier, Franklin D. Roosevelt, officially covering the "Mainbrace" exercise, while up on deck, took 3 excellent color photographs of a large round silvery-white object in the sky above the fleet.
Personal Letter from Wallace Litwin
FLYING SAUCERS, Trend Books, Max Miller, p 75
THE TRUTH ABOUT FLYING SAUCERS, Aime Michel, p 130
THE UFO EVIDENCE, NICAP, p 88-89

27 September 1952, Goteborg, Sweden, 24:00
A UFO was reportedly photographed by an unidentified witness. No other details are available.
IRC Printout, source 9V 0795M, SNI 140

29 September 1952, Operation "Mainbrace", North Sea
For a whole hour a luminous object, "twice as bright as a big star", operated over Scandinavia. It proceeded by irregular jerks, emitting sparks and leaving a trail of "smoke" behind it. Press photographs were taken and published the next day. For several minutes three small "satelites" were seen moving around the main object. There were many, thousands and perhaps tens of thousands of eyewitnesses.
THE TRUTH ABOUT FLYING SAUCERS, Aime Michel, p 134, Plate 25 opp p 163

30 September 1952, Sweden
A meteor-like object moving slowly in the sky over Operation "Mainbrace" was photographed during the North Sea Exercise. The photographer was not identified. No other details are available. A picture was printed in a London daily newspaper.

16 November 1952, Landrum, South Carolina, 17:00
Mr. David Bunch, with J.B.McLean and other witnesses, saw and photographed a group of round glowing objects moving in the sky near the town of Landrum. the 40 feet of 8mm color movie film shot through a telephoto lens shows 5 glowing oval-shaped objects flying in the sky.
THE UFO EVIDENCE, NICAP, p 89

20 November 1952, Desert Center, California
Mr. George Adamski snapped the first photographs of a bell-shaped flying object. The pictures were reportedly taken in view of other witnesses including Rick Williamson, and the film was originally processed for Rick Williamson in Phoenix, Arizona, and were printed in the Phoenix Gazette. Mr. Adamski later called Williamson and asked him to burn the negatives, which he did.

November 1952, Culver City, California, 16:00
MGM Studios produced an official photograph made by Studio Lot #2 of a large disc-shaped object moving in the sky above the camera crew at work on a different kind of movie production. This sighting was real and interrupted the normal shooting.
From a confidential report

1 December 1952, Palomar Gardens, California, 13:30
Mr. George Adamski photographed a dark circular object moving in the sky and leaving a kind of misty trail seen to come from the aft part of the craft.
SAUCERS, Trend Books, Max Miller

13 December 1952, Palomar Gardens, California, 09:00
Mr. George Adamski again shot pictures of the bell-shaped circular craft, taken this time through his 6" homemade telescope.
FLYING SAUCERS HAVE LANDED, Leslie and Adamski

13 December 1952, Palomar Gardens, California
Mr. Jerrold Baker shot a dark picture of a strange bell-shaped circular craft similar to the one seen in the Adamski picture taken shortly before. The object in the Jerrold photo is very low above some tree branches. Only the wide underside is visible as the object nearly fills the image frame. The left part of the object is not in the picture.
Fred Steckling

26 December 1952, Miami, Florida, 01:05
A UFO was reportedly photographed over Miami by an unidentified witness. No other details are available.
IRC Printout, source K 40FL

1952, Valpariso, Chile, Evening
A "V" formation of luminous objects in a dusk sky similar to the UFO formation that later became known as the "Lubbock Lights" was photographed as it flew over the Valpariso Naval Base.
Operazione Plenilono, Renato Vesco, Plate 24

1952, Southeast Asia, Daytime
A bright light colored spherical body was photographed hovering in the sky over troops boarding an HRS-1 Helicopter. A snow-covered mountain is seen in the background.
CBA UFO News, Vol. 6, No. 1 (Spring-Summer) 1974

1952, Catalina Island, California, Daytime
Mr. Bob Jung reportedly took photographs of a UFO from aboard a boat standing off Catalina.

1952, Alaska, Daytime
A circular UFO with a dark center underneath, very much like the UFO photographed over Passiac, New Jersey, was photographed hovering above a seaplane, a Beechcraft 17 biplane on floats, in a small lake inlet in Alaska.
August Roberts collection

. . . . .

1953

19 January 1953, Aguadulce, Panama
A UFO was reportedly photographed by an unidentified witness. No other details are available. This was reported as a suspected hoax but no reason why was given.
IRC Printout, Source 8 40GA 27+

1 February 1953, Albuquerque, New Mexico, 04:00
A UFO was reportedly photographed by a witness identified only as H. No other details are available.
IRC Printout 1 40GA 62

2 February 1953, Victorville, California, 18:00
A UFO was reportedly photographed by a witness identified only as a confidential source. No other details are available.
IRC Printout, source F 40GB 06+

24 February 1953, Olean, New York, 04:00
A UFO was reportedly photographed by an unidentified witness. No other details are available.
IRC Printout, source 4 40GB 81+

3 March 1953, Luke AFB, Phoenix, Arizona, 20:25
Official 16mm gun-camera film was shot of a UFO near Luke AFB. It was filmed from an F-84 jet fighter aircraft. No other details available. The film has not been released by the Air Force. Probably another version of the report below.
IRC Printout, source K 40GC 07+

222

3 March 1953, Luke AFB, Phoenix, Arizona, 13:25 - 13:32
Captain Roderick D. Thompson of the 3600th Fighter Training Group, Luke AFB, leading a flight of 3 F-84 jet interceptor aircraft, encountered, at 25,000 feet and 500 mph, a 300 to 500 foot diameter crescent shaped object flying above them. Thompson gave chase up to 30,000 feet altitude and 560 mph, and when the object began to climb away, he activated his gun camera and shot 30 feet of 16mm movie film of it before it was gone.
Flying Saucer Review, Vol.24, No. 2, 1978, p 11

17 March 1953, Puerto Ordez, Venezuela
A UFO was reportedly photographed by a witness identified only as H.
IRC Printout, source 40GC 37+

4 April 1953, Nomurka, Australia (135 miles north of Melbourne)
An unidentified man waiting at church to take a picture of a bride, noticed a strange conical-shaped UFO maneuvering rapidly in the sky. He turned around and snapped one quite clear picture of the object. It was a very clear day with some scattered clouds standing out white against the blue sky. The witness used a Kodak Retina II camera set at f8 and 1/250th second.
FLYING SAUCERS OVER AUSTRALIA, James Holledge, p 47

6 May 1953
A UFO was reportedly photographed by an unidentified witness at an undisclosed location on this date.
IRC Printout, source 40GE-

16 May 1953, Bouffioulx, Hainaut, Belgium, 20:15
M. Hermann Chermanne snapped 2 black and white photos of a shining metallic flattened circular object hovering over Blandhe Bournf Quarter. The second photograph shows the object "exploding". It had a brilliantly luminous white center with an iris-colored halo around it. When the cloud substance settled to the ground after the explosion, it was found to consist of a white filiamentary material that disappeared in a short time.
IRC Printout, sources M 8M1 182, M 7L1 031M, N 9V 0870M

31 May 1953, Jindabyne, South Australia
A UFP was reportedly photographed by an unknown witness in South Australia. No other details are available.
IRC Printout 7Z2 026

May 1953, Mt. Palomar, California
An anonymous witness reportedly photographed a UFO through an 8" telescope. No other details are available. This may be a confusion of one
oof the Adamski photos although the size of the telescope and dates
do not agree with any known Adamski picture.

17 June 1953, Mallorca, Balearic Islands, Spain
A UFO was reportedly photographed by an unidentified witness. No other
details are available. (Not to be confused with the Enrique Hausmann
Müller photo of 25 March 1950.)
IRC Printout, cource 9V 0872R

26 June 1953, Cuenca, Spain, 07:00
Don Manuel Carlos Ruiz Schick observed and photographed a very large
intensely luminous disc-like object looking like a full moon. A coast
artillery battery estimated the altitude at 45 kilometers. It was at
first seen as an oval shape and then it thinned to a lance-tip shape,
inclined to an oblique position and was seen as a smooth flattened
lens, and then it began to move north. It disappeared in a very few
minutes.
FLYING SAUCERS ANTE LA CAMERA, Antonio Ribera, p 153

2 July 1953, Tinker AFB, Oklahoma, 00:45
A UFO was reportedly photographed by an unidentified witness, No other
details are available.
IRC Printout, sources 8 40GG 02+, 600 531, 4HR 0520

8 August 1953, Bad Hersfeld, Germany, 05:45
Herr Albrecht Steiner observed and photographed a dark disc-shaped
object hovering in the sky at an inclination of about 45 degrees from
the vertical. Three hemi-spherical protrusions are evident on the under side of the craft.

9 August 1953, Moscow, Idaho, 21:23 - 23:37
An estimated 200 foot diameter pinkish-white luminous disc-shaped
object was observed and photographed in the night sky. The round object remained stationary in the north at an estimated 1,000 feet altitude. Then it moved slowly eastward and rose to about 8,000 feet.
A steady white light approached from below and eastward and merged
with the larger light. Four more smaller white lights came from above
and also merged with the object. The whole thing remained until daylight when it was seen as a small bright shiny object getting more and
more distant. (See the report below)
Fate Magazine, May 1954, p 32-36
Probe Magazine, Spring 1967, p 33

10 August 1953, Moscow, Idaho, 17:00
USAF Chief Ground Observer L.E. Towner watched, at 1,500 feet altitude to the south, a brilliant round or circular object moving slowly in the sky. He snapped the last shots on his roll of film of the strange object before it disappeared.
Operazione Plenilune, Renato Vesco, p 20

12 August 1953, Ellsworth AFB, North Dakota
Official Air Force gun-camera film from an F-84 jet fighter aircraft was exposed on an intercept mission from Ellsworth AFB.
George D. Fawcett Research Pamphlet #5
FLYING SAUCERS AND THE U.S. AIR FORCE, Lawrence S. Tacker

12 August 1953, Rapid City, South Dakota
Two USAF jet interceptor fighter aircraft chased and photographed a UFO which then turned and followed the first jet back towards its home base. The film was not released by the Air Force.
SAGA UFO Report, August 1977, p 68
THE UFO EVIDENCE, NICAP, p 89
Galaxy, Vol. 1, No. 3, Ted Zachary (CIA's NPIC reportedly has photos)

23 August 1953, Port MOresby, New Guinea, 11:00
Director of Civil Aviation, Mr. T.P.Drury and his wife observed and photographed a strange UFO that materialized in a clear cloudless sky. Drury was taking movies of a native boy spearing fish when his wife noticed a wisp of cloud forming in the clear sky. Together they stood there and watched it build into a thick white mass of cumulous c;oud. There were no other clouds in the sky at the time. Because of his interest in meteorological phenomena, Drury rotated the telephoto lens of his French movie camera into position and started to film the funny cloud. Suddenly, as they watched, a silvery dart shot out of the cloud and upwards at a steep 45 degree angle. The UFO was elongated, like a bullet, and subtended about 1" at arm's length. It was sharper in the front and appeared truncated at the rear though the tail was partly obscured by a vpor trail. It was metallic and flashed in the sun, and was very clear and sharp visually. No wings or fins were visible. It was traveling at an incredible speed, at least 5 times the speed of a jet plane at the speed of sound. It disappeared going up and away in the clear blue sky. The object was completely silent. The original cloud was at that time about 50 degrees above the horizon to the southwest, towards Napanapa. There was nothing by which to estimate altitude and distance. An almost identical UFO was observed by Mrs. Walter at Cammeray, New South Wales in March of 1966
SAGA UFO Report, August 1977, p 68
FLYING SAUCERS OVER AUSTRALIA, James Hollege

3 September 1953, Portland, Oregon
A UFO was reportedly photographed by an unidentified witness. No other
details are available
IRC Printout, source 40GI 03-

4 Modesto, California, 03:00
Mr. Charles Rogers of Modesto, a newspaper photographer, saw a strange
light in the early morning sky that seemed to remain stationary. He
set his camera up on the roof, left the shutter open for a few seconds
and snapped a good photo of an elliptical yellowish light.
True, Flying Saucers, #1, 1967, p 34

October 1953, North Queensland, Australia
Mr. W.C. Hall photographed a dense-looking tropical-hat-shaped UFO of
circular form with a prominent dome on top as it hovered over a herd
of sheep.

3 November 1953, Norton AFB, California, 04:00
A UFO was reportedly photographed by a witness identified only as J.
No other details are available.
IRC Printout, source J 40GK 04+

14 November 1953, Lebanon, Ohio
A UFO was reportedly photographed by a witness identified only as
Coleman. No other details are available.
IRC Printout, Source 600 54E, 40 GK-

17 November 1953, Chitose Airport, Japan, 10:50
Miss Hatsue Yoshiike observed and photographed a glowing cloud-like
UFO over the tail of an All Nippon Airways jetliner, Flight #51, park-
ed on the loading ramp.
CBA Japanese Flying Saucer News

28 November 1953, Ma-Pa, United States, 18:30
A UFO movie was reportedly filmed by an unidentified witness.
IRC Printout, source 722 0991

Mid-November 1953, Idaho
Lt. Mel Noel claimed he shot 16mm gun camera movies of a UFO from an
F-86 jet fighter which he was piloting. He says he photographed 5 huge
disc-shaped craft 150' - 180' in diameter by 30' to 40' thick. They
were moving at times up to an estimated 3,000 mph.
PLATILLOS VOLANTES EN LA ACTUALIDAD, Eugenio Danyans, p 69

29 December 1953, Paris, France, 03:45
M. Paul Paulin reportedly observed and photographed a bright round light in the sky over Paris.
IRC Printout, sources 7C3 135U, 40 OL, 9V 0922Q

Mid-1953, Cincinnati, Ohio
A UFO was reportedly photographed by an unidentified witness. No other details are available.
IRC Printout, sources 600 54D, 40GE- C, 7LI 0320

1953, Palmdale, California
A Lockheed Aircraft official factory photograph, shot from a T-33 Jet Trainer aircraft on gun camera film, shows a bright round object high in the sky. The photo was taken at extremely high altitude but was too distant for good resolution.
Lucius Farish

1953, Gulf of Mexico
An Air Force Patrol Plane shot official color movie of a number of small disc-shaped objects flying into a huge disc-shaped flying craft.
Confidential report from a crew member

1953, Norfolk, Virginia
Mr. William Turrentine photographed a solid-looking disc-shaped flying object having a form of tri-hemispherical structure underneath.

1953, North Korea
A Marine Corps pilot shot an official Navy photograph, from his jet fighter aircraft in flight, of a clearly outlined solidly opaque disc-shaped craft in flight in close formation with his plane. The object was a light metallic color on top and had a coppery-bronze color underneath. The pilot was not identified.
SPACECRAFT FROM BEYOND THREE DIMENSIONS, Gordon Allen

1953, Australia
Mr. Kevin Power reportedly photographed a UFO over Australia. No other details are available.

1953, Army Factory, near Rio de Janeiro, Brazil, 23:00
A large oval object, obviously a thick disc-form at an angle, reflecting light from the factory below was photographed about 500 to 1,000 feet above the Army Plant. A bank employee observing from the verandah of his home had his wife bring him their camera and he snapped 2 black

227

and white pictures. He then reset the camera and snapped one time exposure of the same object. The first two pictures were badly underexposed but the third shot came out quite well. The whole observation lasted about 10 minutes.
Fate Magazine, September 1960, p 45

Summer 1953, Cincinnati, Ohio, Dawn
An anonymous photographer shot 4 photographs of a 40" octagon-shaped object over the tree-tops of the city. No other details are available.

1953, Ellsworth AFB, South Dakota
A UFO was reportedly photographed by an unidehtified witness. No other details are available. This may be a mis-quote of the 12 August Ellsworth AFB incident.
IRC Printout, source 7E4 242

1953, Hagerstown, Maryland
Mr. Dan Frankforter, official photographer for the Fairchild Aircraft Corporation, snapped a picture of a new C-119 Air Transport taking off, and captured 2 rosey-centered, domed disc-shaped objects in flight high in the background sky.
CBA UFO News, Vol. 6, No. 1 (Spring-Summer) 1974, p 161

End 1953, Vatican City, Rome, Italy
Many photographs were reportedly made of more than a dozen dark disc-shaped UFOs which made a cross formation over the Plaza San Pedro. The formation broke up and pairs of craft and singles cris-crossed over Rome at low and intermediate altitudes.
Platillos Voladores - Il Giornale di Italia, Perez, December 1953

. . . . .

1954

15 January 1954, Alice Springs, Australia, Daylight
An unidentified observer was taking pictures of Mount Gillen when suddenly an enormous 150' circular-looking dark flying object appeared from behind the Mountain. It went higher, then dropped down to come quite low between the mountain and Alice Springs. It was traveling slowly, almost at a hover, when the picture was snapped. It then sped off gaining velocity as it climbed higher and higher into the west. It appeared to have something like heavy "veins" running to the rim.
Confidential Letter
IRC Printout, source 7H5 097

17 January 1954, Snoqualmi Falls, Washington
Photographer Joseph Scayles shot a picture of a winter scene with a strange cloud in the background. Subsequent enlarging and darkening of the print showed a well defined domed disc emitting a lighter trail in the cloud mass in which it was moving.
Verbal report
IRC Printout, Source 5N 66DS

1 February 1954, Tuscaloosa, Alabama, 20:00
A UFO was reportedly photographed by a witness identified only as B. No other details are available.
IRC Printout, source H 40HB 03+

15 February 1954, Tover, England (Conniston Hill), 11:00
Master Stephen Darbisher, 13 years old, and his young cousin, observed and photographed a bell-shaped object hovering over the hilltop. The craft was very similar to an object reportedly photographed by George Adamski on 13 December 1952 although not nearly as clear a picture. This object was a less distinct cloud-like mass photographed with a toy pin-hole camera. The boys were walking up Conniston Hill when they heard a strange buzzing noise over the crown. As they neared the top, the UFO came over it also, in their direction. They snapped one photo before it flew away.
THE RIDDLE OF THE FLYING SAUCERS, Gerald Heard
Real Flying Saucers Pictorial, 1967, p 15, p 55
IRC Printout, source 9 9S 0527W

18 February 1954, Lissimouth, Scotland, 12:35
Mr. Cedrick Allingham reported that he photographed a bright luminous pyramid of light in the clouds above him which turned into a bell-shaped flying object. He estimated the altitude of the craft in the first picture to be about 5,000 feet.
FLYING SAUCERS FROM MARS, Cedric Allingham, p 104, plates face p 32-33

7 March 1954, Mobile, Alabama, 17:30
A UFO was reportedly photographed by an unidentified witness. No other details are available.
IRC Printout, source H 40HC 09+

14 March 1954, Puddingstone Reservoir, California (50 miles N Los An.)
Mr. J.W. Wasker claimed he photographed a fat-flanged disc-shaped object looking something like a hamburger bun flying low over the reservoir.

March, 1954, Rouen, France
A small flat disc-shaped object with a thick antenna or mast of some kind on its top was photographed near Rouen.
IRC Printout, source 7H3 089

11 April 1954, Tokai, South Africa, 14:00
A UFO was reportedly photographed by a witness identified only as Villiers
IRC Printout, source G 5N 54DK

April 1954, New Zealand
The New Zealand Air Force received several strips of movie film of moving points of light in the night skies, but they were unable to trace their origin.
Confidential report

24 May 1954, Dayton, Ohio, 12:00 (15 miles NW)
Official USAF photographs were taken by staff photographer Robert Brubaker from a Boeing B-29 bomber aircraft of a 125'diameter mirror-finish bright round UFO below and behind the B-29. The picture was overexposed but it did capture the flying object. The UFO was estimated to be at 6,000 feet altitude and moving at about 600 mph. It was shot from the 16,000 foot altitude of the bomber.
THE UFO EVIDENCE NICAP, p 89
SAGA UFO Report, August 1977, p 168
THE REPORT ON UNIDENTIFIED FLYING OBJECTS, Edward J. Ruppelt, p 311
Galaxy, Vol. 1, No. 3, Article by Ted Zachary

24 May 1954, Richmond, Indiana, 17:25
Major Leo N. Brubaker shot photographs of a gleaming spherical light mass in an aerial topographical photo taken from high altitude from an Air Fore B-29 on a photo mission. (See the item above, same date)
True, Flying Saucers #1, 1967, p 20
IRC Printout, source M 40HE 24+

24 May 1954, Chicago, Illinois, 23:00
A UFO was reportedly photographed by an unidentified witness. No other details are available.
IRC Printout, source 4 40HE 26+

7 June 1954, Marseilles, France
A thick dark lens-shaped flying object with a light on top and two lights visible near the rim was photographed near Marseilles.
UFO Nachrichten, DUIST, Wiesbaden W. Germany

9 June 1954, Mooresville, Indiana, 21:30
A UFO was reportedly photographed by an unidentified witness. No other details are available.
IRC Printout, source 8 40HF

18 June 1954, Olmstead AFB, Pennsylvania, 11:42
A UFO was reportedly photographed by an unidentified witness. No other details are available.
IRC Printout, source 49HF 24+

21 June 1954, Buffalo, New York, 15:10
A UFO was reportedly photographed by an unidentified witness. No other details are available.
IRC Printout, source 3 5N

26 June 1954, Danville, Illinois, 23:45
A UFO was reportedly photographed by an unidentified witness. No other details are available.
IRC Printout, source 7 40HF 45+

30 June 1954, Keflavik, Iceland, 12:20
Dr. Hallur Hallsson Jr., Dentist, taking pictures of the solar eclipse at timed intervals exposed a whole roll of film of the phenomenon. When the developed prints came back he noticed a distinct luminous round flying object in 4 of the pictures. The bright disc-like object appeared to move tilted up on edge toward the sun from the right, then to drop below the line of sight to the sun and accelerate out of the pictures to the right again. The object is quite clearly seen as a structured form in two of the pictures, and even some detail of the top of the craft is visible. The object was in the near vicinity below the scud clouds and was illuminated or radiant on the near side, away from the sun, which should have been in shadow.
Personal letter from Dr. Hallsson
Flying Saucer Review, May-June 1958, p 7

30 June 1954, Keflavik, Iceland, 12:25
West German tourist K.G. Jensen, visiting Iceland, set up his camera to photograph the solar eclipse. In one of his pictures he captured a bluish-silver metallic-looking object flying in a tilted up on edge attitude, with a structured dome on top. It was below the scud clouds and was illuminated on the near side, which should have been in shadow because the sun was beyond.
From a personal letter from Ole Henningsen of Denmark

30 June 1954, Keflavik, Iceland, 12:30
Mr. Karl Magnusson shot a whole roll of black and white pictures of
the solar eclipse from a beach near Keflavik. The developed pictures
showed luminous images that are believed to be lens-flares from his
shooting directly at the sun.
Flying Saucer Review

30 June 1954, Oslo, Norway, 14:17 (Over Hardangervidde Plateau)
Mr. Johnny Bjornulf and two other newsmen aboard an airliner at 13,000
feet over Lifjeld, observed and photographed two large disc-shaped
circular objects in the air above the airliner to the right. The men
were aboard the plane to photograph the solar eclipse taking place
when the objects were noticed. The time was nearly simultaneous with
the two reports above, the difference in time reported being due to
time zones. The objects were filmed on 16mm color movie film as they
watched the objects fly away.

30 June 1954, Chicago, Illinois
Miss Mildred Maier shot a picture of the solar eclipse that day which
upon development was found to have an image if a UFO in the air.

30 June 1954, Minneapolis, Minnesota
Mr. Marvin Tornham, photographing the solar eclipse on this date, captured a large flat disc-shaped object in the sky in the same frame
with the eclipsing sun.

June 1954, Muskogee, Oklahoma, 14:00
A UFO was reportedly photographed by an unidentified witness. No other
details are available.
IRC Printout, source 1 40HF +

3 July 1954, Bermuda Island
A 35mm movie was filmed of a UFO over the island of Bermuda. No other
details are available.

3 July 1954, Fairchild AFB, Washington, 21:40
A UFO was reportedly photographed by an unidentified witness. No other
details are available.
IRC Printout, source 5 40HG 05+

4 July 1954, BA, 01:42
A UFO was reportedly photographed by an unidentified witness. No other
details are available.
IRC Printout, source 9 40HG 04x

5 July 1954, Sussex, England
Mr. B.V. Simmons observed and photographed a huge multi-tiered deep disc-shaped flying object in the sky. The photograph is indistinct.

18 July 1954, Queensland, Australia
Mr. W.C. Hall reportedly photographed a domed disc-shaped object of a form very similar to a pith-helmet. It was seen above a flock of sheep. (See similar report October 1953)
SIR Magazine, February 1955

30 July 1954, Michigan
Mr. Buck Nelson reported that he had photographed a UFO near his home.

30 July 1954, Mountain View, Missouri
A UFO was reportedly photographed by a Mr. N. No other details are available.
IRC Printout, source 40HG

3 August 1954, Richenstein Mtns., Gesause/Stiermark, Austria, 13:00
Herr Henrich Kaiser snapped a photograph of what appears to be a line of 4 disc-shaped flying objects standing on edge, one behind another. They are in a horizontal formation apparently above the mountainous skyline.

3 August 1954, Australia
Three UFOs were reportedly photographed over central Australia by an unidentified photographer. No other details are available.

5 August 1954, Salisbury, Rhodesia
A remarkably clear sharp photograph was made of a darker, domed, disc-shaped object seen over some public buildings in Salisbury.

2 September 1954, 23:00
Miss Paula Brite, location unidentified, photographed a circular disc-shaped flying object hovering overhead.

9 September 1954, Nelson, New Zealand, 02:20
Mr. K.M. Gibbons and Mr. Alex Ingram observed 3 glowing disc-shaped UFOs in the sky about 5 miles apart. Gibbons took three 35mm photos of the objects as they hovered over a mudflat. They wobbled like tops and glowed a radiant blue-white. Two of the discs tilted on edge and streaked up vertically, then the third brightened and streaked away horizontally. He used a Canon camera with a telephoto lens.
THE UFO EVIDENCE, NICAP, p 89
FLYING SAUCERS UNCENSORED, Harold Wilkins, p 96

233

18 September 1954, Azusa, California, 15:30
Mr. Daniel Fry reported that he snapped a photograph of a small dark metallic hub-shaped object low in the sky, and offered the pictures to prove it.

22 September 1954, Paris, France
A famous writer (who insists on anonymity) living at the foot of the Eiffel Tower, noticed a round luminous, but not bright, object stationary in the sky toward the Arc de Triumpf. It had a saturn-like ring of mist around the middle of it. He got his camera and snapped a picture of it, and then noticed that nobody in the street below was paying any attention to the object in the sky. He put on his coat and went down to join them in the street, to see how long it would take for someone to discover what he still could see. It finally flew away before anyone else seemed to notice it. He became depressed about the insensibility of humanity and went back to his flat.

24 September 1954, Grenoble, S.W. France, 13:06
M. Jacques Baccard observed a dark round UFO leaving a dark trail in the sky as it flew along. He estimated the object to be about eighty meters (nearly 240 feet) in diameter. It was flying along horizontally about 1,200 meters above the ground.
IRC Printout, source 1 9V 1135G

28 September 1954, Stockholm, Sweden
A UFO was reportedly photographed by an unknown witness. No other Details are available.
IRC Printout, source 9V 1182G

29 September 1954, Bjuv, Sweden
A UFO was reportedly photographed by an unidentified witness. No other details are available.
IRC Printout, source 9V 1191M

30 September 1954, Pyrennes Mountains, France
A UFO was reportedly photographed by an unidentified witness. No other details are available.
IRC Printout, source 9S 3073

September 1954, Helsinki, Finland
A huge white disc partly obscured by haze or mist was observed almost directly above through thin clouds over the sity. Another identical white disc-shaped craft of similar huge size was observed through the clouds above and much higher than the first. Both were photographed in the same frame.

1 October 1954, Ambleteuse, France
A UFO was reportedly photographed by an unidentified witness. No other details are available.
IRC Printout, source 9V 1229M

2 October 1954, Boulogne Mer, France, 16:00
A UFO was reportedly photographed by an unidentified witness. No other details are available.
IRC Printout, source 4 9V 1278X

2 October 1954, Ambleterre, North France, Day
M. Emile Turpin observed and photographed a brilliant luminous white oval mass in the daylight sky.
IRC Printout, source 9S 0647Z

4 October 1954, Lagny-Rigollet, France, 04:00
A UFO was reportedly photographed by an unidentified witness. No other details are available.
IRC Printout, source G 9V 1362M

15 October 1954, Anchorage, Alaska, 16:43
Mr. and Mrs. Richard Beaulieu observed a UFO hovering at the edge of a local lake and snapped a picture of it.
Confidential source

15 October 1954, Gyorm Hungary
An anonymous teacher photographed a huge shining reddish-colored object as if flew through the sky at 40 kilometers per minute. It was estimated to be about 200 meters altitude and 1,000 meters distant when the photo was snapped. Over a thousand witnesses observed tthis spectacle. It was only seen in this particular region. Two color photographs were made in all.
UFOs FROM BEHIND THE IRON CURTAIN, Hobana, p 199
TUKOR Weekly for 10 September 1968
The URANIA Astronomical Observatory received 1,500 witness reports.

16 October 1954, Sedan, France, 22:00
A UFO was reportedly photographed by an unidentified witness. No other details are available.
IRC Printout, source B 9V 1679G

20 October 1954, AN 23:45
A UFO was reportedly photographed by an unidentified witness. No other details are available.
IRC Printout, source D 9V 1755X

27 October 1954, Und, Hungary
A teacher who wishes to remain anonymous observed and photographed a disc-shaped flying object in the sky above Und.
Esti-Bud Daily, 27 October 1954
UFOs FROM BEHIND THE IRON CURTAIN, Hobana, p 201
IRC Printout, source 9V 1820G

24 October 1954, Boulogne-Sur-Mer, Pas de Calais, France, 17:00
About 7 kilometers from Boulogne-Sur-Mer, M. Emile Turpin (34), Railroad Inspector for SNCF, saw a bright reflective metallic disc of a bronze-like color fly a curved course at 50 degrees elevation descending to 30 degrees, then it made a sharp turn and ascended vertically and disappeared. Turpin was able to obtain 2 black and white photos during the short observation. His camera was a Foca Standard set at f5.6 and f6.3 at 1/100th second on Tri-X film.
LDLN November 1973, Nr. 129, p 16, 17 and cover.

24 October 1954, Hungary
A schoolmaster reportedly observed and photographed an UFO. No other details are available.

29 October 1954, Olmstead AFB, Pennsylvania, 22:20
An UFO was reportedly observed and photographed by an unidentified witness. No other details are available.
IRC Printout, source D 40HJ 46+

2 November 1954, Malaga, Spain
Sr. Juan Coll and Jose Antonio saw and photographed a dark circular disc-shape in the sky over some mountains.
IRC Printout, sources 9V 1874M, 9V 1874G

4 November 1954, Florence, Italy, Night
Prof. Maria Romoli, in the presence of other witnesses, took close-up pictures of a "flaming" UFO. No other details are available.

6 November 1954, Padre Island, Texas, 23:00
Mr. Ray Stanford and his brother Rex and a couple of friends observed and photographed an orange colored, flattened, low profile, flat domed disc-shaped object hovering over the sand of the beach there. Rays of light came from the left side of the rim and the cupola.
Personal Letter from Ray Stanford

6 November 1954, Rome, Italy, 11:00
Sgn. Turi Mattarella took a photograph of a double domed lens-shaped

object over Monte Mario, a hill on the Tiber River in Rome. No other details are available.

9 November 1954, Wilcannia, S.W. Australia
A UFO was reportedly photographed by an unidentified witness from the town of Wilcania. No other details are available.
IRC Printout, source 9V 1984G

14 November 1954, Ponchartrain, York, England
A UFO was reportedly photographed by an unidentified witness. No other details are available.
IRC Printout, source 9V 1995M

18 November 1954, Cuba, 07:31
An unidentified witness reportedly observed and photographed a UFO over Cuba. No other details are available.
IRC Printout, source 0 40HK 32+

November 1954, Taormina, Scicily
Two cloudlike UFOs were observed and photographed against a sky background as people in the foreground appear to be watching the objects in the sky. This photograph was investigated by the United States Embassy and the picture was brought to the U.S.A. by Ambassador Clare Booth Luce.

6 December 1954, Madison, Wisconsin, 21:57
A witness identified only as H. reportedly photographed a UFO over the city of Madison. No other details are available.
IRC Printout, source G 40HL 08+

9 December 1954, Rio de Janeiro, Brazil, 23:00
A witness identified only as F.C. took 3 photographs of a bright disc-shaped object flying in the sky. The 1st and 2nd photos are underexposed. The object was photographed over a munitions plant in Rio. It hung motionless in a windy sky, reflecting the lights of the plant below. It suddenly took-off at high speed and disappeared.
Flying Saucers, UFO Reports No. 1, 1967, p 47
IRC Printout, sources K 6AO 58HF, K 9S 0867A

10 December 1954, El Tigre, Venezuela, Day
An American engineer shot a picture of 5 UFOs flying in formation.
IRC Printout, sources 9PP, 8A1 050

16 December 1954, Victorville, California, 18:00 - 11:00 next day
Hundreds of witnesses at Apple Valley, many with cameras, observed a large cigar-shaped object hovering in the sky over Apple Valley for hours. The object seemed to be made of very bright silvery metallic material. It remained stationary at about 25,000 feet almost directly above the Apple Valley Inn. It appeared as a reddish glow at noght, reddish to reddish-orange. It became silvery bright again in the daylight next morning. It was estimated to be over 2½ times the size of a B-29, and looked like it had two large ports at one end near the bottom. All photographs reported were confiscated by local authorities and were not returned. We suspect that there are still some of these photos out there that were not reported, and may still be in the hands of the original photographers. We hope to hear from some of them.
FLYING SAUCERS, Trend Books, Max Miller, p 85

31 December 1954, Peseux, Switzerland, 07:55
An unidentified witness known only as V. reportedly obtained a photograph of a UFO over Peseux. No other details are available.
IRC Printout, source 2 4UDJ 02Z

December 1954, Wolverhampton, England
Mr. Harold Cummings, 16 years old, obtained a picture of a dark disc-shaped object hovering low in the sky. No other details are available.

December 1954, Wednesfield, England
A witness identified only as Cummings reportedly took a photograph of a UFO. No other details are available. This report is believed to be another version of the previous report described above.
IRC Printout, source 7J2 102

1954, Australia
A movie sequence of an UFO was reportedly filmed on easter Sunday by an unidentified witness. No other details are available.
IRC Printout, source 6FO 69E

1954. Wilcania, NSW, Australia
A UFO was photographed following the vapor contrail of a jetliner in flight. The photographer was unidentified. No other details are available on the location, time, etc.
Australian Flying Saucer News

1954, South Africa
Mr. Ken Rathyen furnished a picture series showing a domed disc-shaped UFO over the buildings of a city. The photographer was not identified.

238

1955

1955 was a year of lull after the heavy UFO activity of 1954 that, though worldwide, seemed to be centered over the Iberian Peninsula and the upper Mediterranean. The year started off slowly but then began to pick up and became fairly active again but lacked a focal center as seemed to be the case for the year before.

. . . . .

31 January 1955, Mount Fuji, Japan, 13:33
An unidentified witness reportedly photographed a UFO in the sky near Mt. Fuji. No other details are available.
IRC Printour, source B 40IA 28+

15 February 1955, New York City, 07:45
A UFO was reportedly photographed by a witness identified only as one Mr. L. No other details are available.
IRC Printout, source 6 40IB 20+

8 March 1955, Broadway, Virginia
Amature astronomer, Mr. Lonzo Dove observed and photographed a round luminous object near the apparent edge of the Moon.
George D. Fawcett Research Pamphlet #5

12 March 1955, Yucca Valley, California, afternoon
Mr. Orville H. Mitchell photographed 4 self-luminous arrowhead-shaped objects in a cloud in the daylight sky. He shot 2 black and white photographs of the 4 objects. Saucers Magazine reported that Mitchell of San Fernando, visiting a spacecraft convention at Giant Rock, saw several small clouds that appeared and disappeared in a clear blue sky. He snapped two pictures of one of the clouds without a filter and two more with a filter installed over the lens. The four delta shaped objects appeared in both shots taken through the filter whereas the witness saw only a cloud with the naked eye. Mitchell used a 4"x5" Speed Graphic camera with a Wollensak Raptar f4.7 coated lens and a Wrattan A filter, and took the pictures on Super-X film.
SAUCERS, Vol. III - No. 3, Sept 1955, Cover and p15

27 March 1955, Fort Lamy, France, 21:00-21:35
An unidentified witness photographed a brilliant luminous flying object in the sky, which was estimated to be over 300 feet in diameter by 120 feet tall. No other details are available.

April 1955, Sahara Desert, French Missile Base
A French government official photographer at the Missile Base in the
Sahara observed and photographed two brightly luminous flying objects
traversing a clear blue sky overhead. The object in the center of the
photograph is the more distant, and is seen as a bright point of light
in the daylight sky. The nearer flying object is seen as a sharply
defined metallic domed-disc with a bright halo of light or substance,
possibly a corona of energy, around it.
SOUCOUPES VOLANTES, Garreau, p70-71

21 May 1955, Plattsburg, New York, 02:15
A witness identified only as Roddy reportedly photographed a UFO over
Plattsburg. No other details are available.
IRC Printout, source C 7J2 182

15 May 1955, Union Square, New York, mid-morning
Mr. Warren Siegmond and a lady friend, a secretary at the United Na-
tions, taking pictures on the roof of an apartment building, noticed a
bright translucent spheroid moving in the sky. It slowed and began
hovering over some nearby buildings as it changed from a radiantly
luminous appearance to a dark solid-looking metallic disc. They watched
it for about 2½ minutes as Siegmond snapped 5 pictures of it before it
became luminous again and flew away.
FSR, Vol. 1, No. 3, Jul-Aug 1955, p2-4

5 June 1955, Namur, Belgium, 19:30
M. Francois Myldermans, an equipment repairman, observed a brightly
luminous flying body as it streaked in, stopped, and hovered in the
sky, becoming a "bottle-green" metallic thick disc-shape. Then it began to move horizontally as it emitted a white trail of substance,
made a flat 360 degree circle, and entered the obscuring trail. When
the trail began to dissipate and dissolve, the object accelerated and
sped away as a streak once more.
Inforespace 2-1, p25

14 July 1955, Madrid, Spain, 19:35
A witness identified only as W. reportedly photographed a UFO over the
Madrid vicinity. No other details are available.
IRC Printout, source 4 40IG 29+

17 July 1955, Draakensburg Range, Natal, South Africa, 11:00
Mrs. Elizabeth Klarer, a housewife, reportedly snapped 7 black and
white photographs of a solid-looking metallic domed disc of a silvery
color as it flew erratically about in the clouds over the Draakensburg

Mountains. It reportedly hovered, landed, took-off again and rose up
through the clouds to disappear from view. Klarer was alone at the
time and was carrying a small box camera. She claimed a contact with
the space pilot during the landed phase of this sighting event.
FSR, Nov-Dec 1956, Vol. 2, No. 6, p2-5

5 August 1955, Anchorage, Alaska
Mr. Gordon Henning observed a round metallic globe in flight in the
sky and photographed it as it was discharging something or leaving a
trail of some kind of substance behind it.

30 August 1955, Didignac, Argentina, 09:30
Sr. Pedro Francisco Navarro went out to take a picture of the front of
his house when he heard a sound like a whirlwind coming from a strange
cloud above. A part of the cloud within the lenticular mass was re-
volving separately. Thinking it a rare meteorological phenomenon, he
raised his camera and snapped a picture. As the clouds moved, he could
see a disc-shaped object within them. The processed negative verified
the photographer's statement.
Aeronautica, January 1956, p25
Espacio, Ano 2, No. 2, 1969, p13
UN ENIGMA ACTUAL, Uriondo, p95
Cuarta Dimension, No. 26, p41

30 August 1955, Old Greenwich, Connecticut, 21:30
A UFO was reportedly photographed over Old Greenwich, Connecticut this
night. No other details are available
IRC Printout, source E 40IH 52+

August 1955, Berlin, West Germany
Herr Christian Schwarzer reportedly photographed 3 shiny disc-shaped
objects flying edge-on to the witness. No other details are available.

3 September 1955, Hiawatha, Iowa, 15:00
Two luminous or bright cloud-like disc-shaped objects were photographed between the observer and the ground of the outskirts of the town
below from an aircraft in flight. No other details are available.

22 September 1955, Hickham AFB, Hawaii, 19:30
A UFO was reportedly photographed by an unidentified witness. No other
details are available.
IRC Printout, sources I 610 56B, 610 56A, I 41

5 September 1955, Cabras Island, Santos, Brazil, 18:00
Dr. Achilles Greco of the Brazilian Navy and some companions, returning from a recreational fishing trip, observed and photographed a very
strange cloud moving independently of the other clouds in the sky that
day, which seemed to be following the boat in to its port. The cloud
began to dissipate revealing a huge disc-shaped metallic craft inside.
Greco snapped one picture of the phenomenon.
IRC Printout, source 4011

September 1955, Philadelphia International Airport, Pennsylvania
Mr. James Mellodew reportedly shot 16mm movie footage of a UFO over
the International Airport. No other details are available.

September 1955, Basel, Switzerland
Eight disc-shaped flying objects were reportedly photographed over the
Ciba, A.G. factory. No other details are available.

23 October 1955, Grand Rapids, Michigan, 00:23
A UFO was reportedly photographed by a witness identified only as O.
No other details are available.
IRC Printout, source 40IJ 35+

25 November 1955, Lomax, Illinois, 23:05
A UFO was reportedly photographed by an unidentified witness. No other
details are available.
IRC Printout, source 40IK 28+

1 December 1955, Ingersoll District, Toronto, Canada
The Huron Clark family observed and photographed a noiseless, circular
black ring with a transparent center as it moved along in the sky. No
other details are available.

31 December 1955, La Boisse, France
A UFO was reportedly photographed by an unidentified witness. No other
details are available.
IRC Printout, source 9V 2059 Q

1955, Little America, Wyoming
A witness identified only as M. reportedly photographed a UFO. No other
details are available.
IRC Printout, source 40IC 01+

1955, Japan
A solid-looking dark, domed, disc-shaped flying object was photographed

in the distance from beneath a tree limb seen in the foreground.

1955, Hamburg, Germany
Six UFOs were photographed flying above some trees. No other details
are available.
IRC Printout, source 40I

1955, Chicago, Illinois
A UFO was reportedly photographed by an unidentified witness. No other
details are available.
IRC Printout, source 40 IA 30+

1955, Newcastle, Wyoming
Mr. William C. Lamb of Newcastle observed and photographed 5 disc-
shaped flying objects soaring in a straight line about 300 feet below
the top of Devil's Tower, seen from the west.

. . . . .

1956

8 January 1956, Robertson Island, Weddell Sea, Chilean Antarctica
An official Chilean Government scientific team observed at length and
photographed, two huge cigar-shaped flying objects standing vertically
on end in the Arctic sky. They were estimated to be about 460 feet
long by 80 feet in diameter. They changed positions, moved fast and
slow, made sharp angular changes in direction, and changed colors as
they maneuvered about. Then they resumed their vertical position again
as the whole scientific team watched. Many photographs in both black
and white and color were were obtained of those objects by the team.
The strange objects remained in the area and were observed by the team
for over two days. The scientists estimated the objects to be operating at an average altitude of about 30,000 feet. They reported these
objects to other scientific stations in their area who also confirmed
watching them.
FSR, Vol. 14, No. 2, Mar-Apr 1968, p20-21

25 January 1956, Beltsville, Maryland, 02:07
A witness identified only as E. reportedly photographed a UFO over
Beltsville. No other details are available.
IRC Printout, source 40JA 27+

8 February 1956, Waikiki, Hawaii, 21:55
Sergeant William Wannall on duty in Hawaii, observed a strange moving

243

light in the night sky there. He took his camera and snapped one photo of the unusual object. When he received the picture back from developing, he was surprised to see that he had in fact photographed 3 moving lights in formation, each of a different color. They had to have been moving at a fantastic speed to have traveled the indicated distance in the short time his camera shutter was open during this fraction second exposure.
IRC Printout, source 7W3 023

19 February 1956, Orly Field, Paris, France, 10:50
An unidentified Flying Object, first seen on RADAR by the control tower, was thought to be an airplane of 4-engine size. Failing to establish radio contact, the control tower asked a Paris-London flight to look out for the craft. That pilot spotted the object and reported a large bright spherical object and described its altitude, which was then observed by the tower controllers. It was an enormous round object shining with a rosey-white luminosity.
OBIETTIVO SUGLI UFO, Turris - Fusco, p127

16 February 1956, West New York City, New Jersey, 11:00
Mr. Bert Buhler observed and photographed 3 large glowing sausage-shaped masses in the daylight sky. They were moving fast and he only had time to snap two pictures before they were gone. The prints that are usually shown have been darkened to bring out the luminous bodies.

13 March 1956, Barquisimeto, Venezuela, 07:30
A witness identified only as D. reportedly observed and photographed an unidentified flying object. No other details are available.
IRC Printout, source 4OJC 17

15 March 1956, Salta, Argentina
A number of unidentified witnesses reportedly took photographs of a large cigar-shaped flying object in the sky above Salta. No other details are available.

21 March 1956, Cincinnati, Ohio
An anonymous news photographer observed and photographed a bluish-white light of intense luminosity as he observed it at a 30 degree angle above the horizon. It revolved slowly in the sky. The light seemed to change form as it revolved. It moved away to the northwest frowing smaller and dimmer as it withdrew until it was gone. The observation lasted 45 minutes.

23 March 1956, Mexico City, Mexico
Astronomer Roberto Ozomo observed and photographed a cylinder-shaped
UFO with abruptly squared ends, very similar to the one photographed
at Cumberland, Rhode Island, by Joseph L. Ferriere on 3 July 1967.
L'AVIAZIONE DI ALTRI PIANETI, Perego, p156

25 March 1956, East Gary, Indiana, 01:20
A UFO was reportedly photographed by an unidentified witness known
only as C. No other details are available.
IRC Printout, source 40JC 32+

March 1956, Arcadia, California
Mr. John A. Moore reportedly photographed a large translucent disc-
shaped UFO flying in the sky.

6 April 1956, Jersey City, New Jersey
Mr. Michael Aurelio observed and photographed a round luminous flying
object in the sky. No other details are available.

14 April 1956, Manomet, Massachussetts
WAC Miss Dorothy Currier saw and photographed a dome-topped saucer-
shaped flying object which had rotating lights, landing gear extended,
and made a humming sound. The pictures were made in the presence of
many witnesses.
George D. Fawcett Research Pamphlet #5

18 April 1956. Salta, Argentina
The National Police reportedly photographed a UFO over Salta. No other
details are available.

21 April 1956, Luanda, Angola
Astronomer C.M. Bettencourt, observing the Moon through a small telescope, saw 8 luminous objects enter the eyepiece from the left pro-
ceeding towards the Moon's position in the sky. He estimated them to
be over 500 kilometers distant and 200 to 300 meters in diameter. He
used a Butenshon 64X Telescope, holding his camera to the eyepiece.
OPERAZIONE PLENILUNA, Renato Vesco, p298, photo 18

April 1956, High Bridge, North Carolina, 22:00-23:00
An unidentified witness reportedly snapped candid camera shots of a
UFO near High Bridge. No other details are available.

May 1956, Charles River, Massachussetts
A UFO was reportedly photographed by an unidentified witness. No other

detaila are available.
IRC Printout, source 40JE 01+

26 June 1956, Flugplatz, Switzerland
Herr Hans Studer reportedly photographed a UFO in flight. No other
details are available.
UFO SIGHTINGS OVER SWITZERLAND, Lou Zinsstag, p48, photo #8

June 1956, Prairie, Texas
Mrs. R.B. shot pictures of 2 solid-looking disc-shaped flying objects
near telephone wires. No other details are available.

10 July 1956, Escondido, California, 10:00
Mr. Harold Huntman photographed a mysty white disc-shaped flying object estimated to be 200 feet in diameter as it hovered over his back
yard. After he snapped the picture it zoomed out of sight in 10 or
less seconds. He claimed "portholes" could be seen in the original
print.
UFOs A PICTORIAL HISTORY, Knight, p85

19 July 1956, Locarno, Switzerland
A solid looking dark saturn-shaped flying object was reportedly photographed by an unidentified witness. No other details are available.

19 July 1956, Wichita, Kansas
Mr. Jim Nelson photographed a bright disc in the daylight sky. No
other details are available.
FLYING SAUCERS, FACT OR FICTION, Trend Books, Max Miller, p114

19 July 1956, San Bernardino, California, 14:30
Mr. Mike Savage observed and photographed a large disc-shaped flying
object. No other details are available.

24 July 1956, Singapore, Malaya, 20:20
Dr. J.L. Bennett, a physician, saw and photographed mysterious lights
in the sky over the city. The developed prints showed a bright patch
of light and two smaller luminous dots of light nearby.
SAGA UFO Report, Summer '75. p32 Also Straits Times.
IRC Printout, source 7A4 073

24 July 1956, Pretoria, South Africa
Mr. Edgar Sievers reportedly observed and photographed a UFO over the
city of Pretoria.
IRC Printout. source 40JG 50

246

July 1956, Cairo, Egypt
A UFO was reportedly photographed by an unidentified witness. No other details are available.
IRC Printout, source 40JG 01+

2 August 1956, Amarillo, Texas.
A UFO was reportedly photographed by an unidentified witness. No other details are available.
IRC Printout, Sources 6NO 58A, 40JH-, 40JG 72X

2 August 1956, High Bridge, North Carolina, 00:45
An unidentified witness snapped a night Polaroid shot of a UFO. No other details are available.

3 August, 1956, Clinton, North Carolina
An unidentified witness reportedly snapped a Polaroid picture of a UFO in the area. No other details are available. This may be a confused report of the item above.

5 August 1956, High Bridge, North Carolina
An unidentified photographer snapped 3 Polaroid prints of an unidentified flying object.

10 August 1956, Cunningham, Tennessee
A witness identified only as M. reportedly snapped pictures of a UFO. No other details are available.
IRC Printout, source 40JH 34+

25 August 1956, Newburg, New York, 10:50
A witness identified only as S. reportedly snapped pictures of a UFO. No other details are available.
IRC Printout, source 40JH 91+

23 August 1956, Dallas, Texas, 05:00
A movie of a UFO was reportedly filmed by a witness identified only as R. No other details are available.
IRC Printout, source 40JH 95+

23 August 1956, Vancouver (near MacLeod), Alberta, Canada, 18:20
Canadian Air Force Commander R.J. Childerhose, flying a CF-100 jet fighter at 20,000' altitude, photographed a sharply defined loaf-shape white body in the cloud tops slightly below him.
Canadian UFO Report

30 August 1956, New Brunswick, New Jersey
Mr. Laszlo Matyasovszky, 14 years old, snapped one photo of a fast-moving disc-shaped UFO in the sky. It was a shiny metallic silver in color with a brilliant red cupola on top. The contrast in this photo is poor.

August 1956, Amarillo, Texas
A diamond-shaped UFO leaving a green trail was photographed high in the afternoon sky. The altitude reached was estimated at about 15,000' above sea level.

6 September 1956, Coos Bay, Oregon, 21:00
A witness identified only as L. reportedly photographed a UFO over the Coos Bay area. No other details are available.
IRC Printout, source 40JI 25+

18 September 1956, Joshua Tree-Yucca Valley, California, 13:00
Mr. Ray Stanford shot 6 feet of 8mm movie film of jet aircraft chasing a glowing light high in the sky. The object appeared to be a very big spherical craft very high up, eluding two jets that were leaving contrails - so high that the jets can not be seen except for the contrail tracks, but the sphere is clearly visible and many times the size of the jet aircraft.
THE UFO EVIDENCE, NICAP, p89
Saucers, Autumn 1958
LOOK UP, Ray Stanford

September 1956, Baja California
Mr. George Adamski filmed 16mm movie footage of two very large round UFOs in close formation flight high in the clear blue sky.
Saucers, Max Miller

October 1956, Newington, Connecticut
A witness identified only as G. reportedly photographed a UFO in the sky above Newington. No other details are available.
IRC Printout, source 40JJ 01+

10 October 1956, Twin Peaks, San Francisco, California, 12:30
Mr. Joe Kerska, a commercial photographer, was on Twin Peaks making a panoramic shot of San Francisco when he heard a humming noise. He then looked up to see a wide disc with a dome on top pass low overhead. He was too amazed to change his camera position in time to get a picture, and was bemoaning his misfortune when another identical craft came overhead. This time he quickly reset and repositioned his camera in

time to get one photograph of the UFO going away. The first craft is still barely visible in the distance towards the far shoreline in this photograph.

14 October 1956, Cincinnati, Ohio
A witness identified only as Baston reportedly shot a picture of a UFO over the city. No other details are available
IRC Printout, sources 7C1 071C, 40JJ 28+, 6CO 56L

10 October 1956, Bostonia, California, 21:00
A witness identified only as H. reportedly photographed a UFO above Bostonia. No other details are available.
IRC Printout, source 40JJ 37+

6 November 1956, Vatican City, Rome, Italy
Hundreds of disc-shaped UFOs flew back and forth over the Vatican for an extended period of time. They flew in various formations including that of a cross at one time. There were hundreds of witnesses.
CBA News

7 November 1956, Los Angeles, California, 20:40
Mr. Richard Veloz took two photographs of a brilliant luminous UFO hovering in the sky above his home. No other details are available.

25 November 1956, 25 Miles E of Pierre, North Dakota, 24:45
Patrolmen Don Kelmand and Jacl Peters observed and photographed a red luminous half sphere hovering at 50' to 100' above the ground. The UFO followed the patrol car as it left the scene.
Private source

29 December 1956, White Pass, Washington, AM
An unidentified flying object was reportedly photographed by a witness identified only as Reed. No other details are available.
IRC Printout, source 7Z2 028

1956, Jersey City, New Jersey
Mr. Robert Stevens reportedly photographed 6 spherical objects of a luminous appearance as they flew along in a shifting and constantly changing formation in the night sky. Their apparent size was much larger than the brightest stars visible at that time.
Confidential private source

1956, Wilcania, NSW, Australia
Mr. John Gregory observed and snapped two pictures of a strange disc-

shaped flying object with a high dome on top as it passed quite low in
the sky above Wilcania. He reported it to authorities and they came
and confiscated the first photo thinking that was all. He did not tell
them he had taken a second photo also, and did not lose it.
Barrier Truth, Broken Hill, NSW, 10 June 1966
Australian Flying Saucer News.

1956, Wilcania, NSW, Australia
   An unidentified man, sighting a bell-shaped craft in flight over a
field near Wilcania, shouted to his wife, "Quick, get my camera." He
shot two photos of the UFO hovering stationary in the sky. He used an
old box camera with a slow shutter speed. He was shaking so badly with
nervous excitement that he got jiggle blurring of the picture.(This is
another report of the item above.)
BDT, 10 June 1966

1956, North Polar Sea
A submarine UFO emerged from the North Polar Sea, hovered above the
surface momentarily, and then flew away as it rose high into the air
and disappeared.
Confidential source

   That concludes out chronology through 1956. Any reader having information on any other UFO photographs made during this time period, or
sho has corrections or additions to the reports shown here, are urged
to get in touch with the publishers for possible update of files. Any
updating information received will be published in future volumes in
this series.

NOTES

NOTES

NOTES

NOTES

NOTES

OTHER BOOKS AVAILABLE FROM THE SAME PUBLISHER

UFO CONTACT FROM RETICULUM, Stevens-Herrmann
  416 Pages, Illustrated $16.95

UFO CONTACT FROM PLANET IARGA, Denaerde-Stevens
  363 Pages, Illustrated   15.95

UFO CONTACT FROM UNDERSEA, Sanchez-Stevens
  190 Pages, Illustrated   14.95

UFO CONTACT AT PASCAGOULA, Mendez-Hickson
  174 Pages, Illustrated   14.95

UFO CONTACT OVER MODERN CHINA, Stevens-Dong
  352 Pages, Illustrated   16.95

UFO CONTACT FROM PLANET KOLDAS, Van Vlierden
  305 Pages, Illustrated   15.95

UFO ABDUCTION AT MIRASSOL, Buhler-Pereira-Pires
  416 Pages, Illustrated   16.95

UFO CONTACT FROM PLANET UMMO, Ribera-Stevens
  354 Pages, Illustrated (each Vol. 1 and Vol. 2)   16.95

UFO CONTACT FROM ITIBI-RA, Pallmann-Stevens
  286 Pages, Illustrated   14.95

UFO CONTACT FROM PLANET ACART, Berlet
  224 Pages, Illustrated,   14.95

UFO CRASH AT AZTEC, Steinman
  254 Pages, Illustrated   15.95

Books may be ordered directly from the publisher. Add $1.25 for mailer
and postage in USA. Add .50 more for foreign, sent via book-rate Post.

UFO PHOTO ARCHIVES
P.O. Box 17206
Tucson, Arizona 17206
U.S.A.